This Book is for

C000149553

You want to let go of pain and peace, love and joy.

The contents of 'The Difference' is applicable to both your personal and your workplace life. As the work of 'mindfulness becomes more recognised, the solutions to the following statements becomes all the more paramount.

- You want answers to the questions that deeply drive you
- You seek to know your real identity
- You seek to understand the deeper mysteries of your spirituality
- You recognise you want healing
- You want to elevate your self-esteem and self-love to become more confident
- You want lightness of well-being to increase your productivity instead of anxiety, depression and stress
- You want confidence to overcome bullying, peer pressure and intimidation
- You want to forgive and be forgiven
- You want to know why you feel love eludes you.
- You're afraid to voice your wants despite knowing that your voice matters
- You need healing from abuse in all its forms
- You need self acceptance to stop the pattern of self sabotage

This list is by no means exhaustive. It is for the one who truly seeks the path to one of wholeness, freedom and abundance so that you can excel in all areas of your life.

What people are saying

Lisa Nichols refers to Valerie's 'Eve's Story' as written in The Blind Spot as **'phenomenal'**. It's a story reminding us that 'determination, resiliency and perseverance is yours to access'... so that 'we can experience the extraordinary life'

Lisa Nichols
Motivational Speaker
Featured in The Secret, Oprah, CNN, Dr Phil, Larry King Live, Steve Harvey Show

Valerie Campbell is an enlightened soul whose experience and work serves to simplify and explain some of life's great complexities. She writes from a place of experience that resonates with us all. I highly recommend her latest work.

Doctor Bishop Wayne Malcolm
Senior Pastor ICAN Ministries

"A thought provoking and often inspiring work that looks at the challenges of navigating through life from a spiritual perspective."

Donley Jack
Programme Director of Applied Criminology, Canterbury Christ Church University

Valerie is also the Author of She's Got That Vibe. 'You have a secret power and this book shows you how to harness and use it! 'She's Got That Vibe' uncovers an age-old secret. So brace yourself to be enlightened!

Raymond Aaron
New York Times Best-Selling Author, Branding Small Business for Dummies, One of the very few filmed for The Secret

Valerie is such an inspirational speaker. She really does leave you wanting more. Refreshing, aspirational with such clarity in her delivery. A great speaker overall.

Elaine Rhule
Founder of Designer Cakes of London

After reading The Difference I realised that Valerie was touching a subject that many of us who have become successful and those who have not become successful attack every day and that is 'self sabotage'. This book allows you and forces you to focus on self-discovery. This book is a master-piece. I love her methodology on how she goes from the spiritual to the physical and makes it such an easy read.

Bennie Randall Jr
CEO Bshani Radio App/Investor

Valerie teaches that stillness of the mind enables us to hear our spiritual expression, which views the world through a different lens. This creates space for empathy, compassion and understanding in our relationships with others, without diminishing our authentic self.

Lorna Pamela Stewart
Multi-award Winning Business and Leadership Consultant and Mentor, CEO LEAP Consortium

Acknowledgements

This book was made possible directly from conversations with God's Spirit and His teachings gleaned from a range of resources; The Bible, A Course in Miracles (The Peace Foundation) The Four Agreements (Don Miguel Ruiz) Loving What Is (Byron Katie) Bishop Wayne Malcolm, ICAN Ministries AND many other influencers on my path, too many to mention. To which I remain eternally grateful.

Much gratitude to my mother, Evelyn Campbell; she deserves a line here, all on her own. She is the strongest woman I know.

Much gratitude to Pastor David; who graphic designed my front cover, who brought God's visual idea to life, patiently dealing with my revisions until I felt it just right.

Thank you to Dwayne Miller for the alternative title 'Perspective'..

Thank you to Carol Nzekwu and Elaine Rhule for simple, spiritual and profound words of encouragement and Donley Jack for his zeal for truth!

A special mention to Phillip Fashanu for 'seeing me' and Denise Dje Komenan for 'listening' to my thoughts every morning!

Thank you to every person who I have ever coached, who unknowingly taught me and to my daughter Imani who God sent to test me to bring me to a place of grounded peace.

Last and not least, I thank in advance, all those who have been assigned in this undertaking to bring this message to millions. In God, do we place our trust. To God Be The Glory.

Dedication

For my granddaughter MIA, my little angel,
so she shall know, the 'I AM' is not just in
her name, but also in her AIM.

VALERIE A. CAMPBELL

THE
Difference

To Know The Difference
is To Be Free!

VALERIE A. CAMPBELL

16, Croydon Road, Beddington,
Croydon , Surrey. CR0 4PA

www.filamentpublishing.com
email: info@filamentpublishing.com
+44 (0) 20 8688 2598

The Difference by Valerie A. Campbell
ISBN 978-1-913192-92-1

© Valerie A Campbell 2020

The right to be recognised as the author of this
work has been asserted by Valerie Campbell in
accordance with the Designs and Copyrights
Act 1988 Section 77

All rights reserved
No portion of this work may be copied in any
way without the prior written permission
of the publishers.

Printed by 4Edge

Table of Contents

Preface

A **Message to Millions**...you don't have to share my Christian faith to receive this message, this message is for the benefit of us all – no exception.

I believe everyone has the right to express their unique voice, I believe in non-conformity, I believe you were born to stand out and you don't need permission to make your potential visible.

I invite you to discover the difference in the glass and as I release this message into the atmosphere, I pray that like a well-aimed arrow it will surely hit its mark and in the wake of its landing, a vast tree will grow and give blossom to fruits of inner peace, love and freedom.

To God Be The Glory

Introduction
Time to live at cause and not effect...

Unfortunately, we live in a society where we often care more about the judgement of our contemporaries... keeping up with the Joneses, which is to the detriment of our society. We only have to look at social media for evidence of this.

The judgements we embrace growing up are completely predicated on the framework that our parents, television, news media, music, radio, teachers, church, government and community leaders feed us and so subsequently, the judgements we communicate, especially to our nearest and dearest, influence and most often stifle their potential and inhibit that which seeks to naturally emerge.

I look at social media and I see fear where people present themselves as masks, hiding for fear of judgement; in denial of their true self and self-worth. Abandoning the freedom to show up as God originally intended.

Too many people are concerned about other people's criticism which hold them back in their daily life, whether it be their personal relationship, romantic or business life. In our society, where has freedom of speech gone? Where has true opinion gone? Freedom is no longer about being free to **'voice your truth'**.

Entire lives have been hampered by a fear of judgement, that their voice doesn't matter. Graveyards are full of the untapped talent of those who never realised their potential and those held back by the negative judgement of themselves and others.

In this day and age, we see bullying in and outside of classrooms, from the child to the adult as people inflict their negative opinion on others... which, in some cases, has led to untimely deaths.

'Let he who is without sin, cast the first stone...' (John 8:7) springs to mind.

This book is for both the offender and the offended and will help transform mind-sets as we must overcome our fears of judgement so we can allow our true authentic self to emerge and be a gift to others.

In the past, I have been a by-product of what other people thought, letting the negative judgements and values, inflicted upon me especially in the form of abuse at a very young age, impact my life. This was until a spiritual encounter in my early 20s gifted me with a 'Method' that caused me to see myself in a whole new way; it is this **that I will break down in this book.**

In this book, there are many methods... ways, approaches to a freer life.

'In My Father's house are many rooms. If it were not so, would I have told you that I am going there to prepare a place for you?' (John 14:2)

I draw an analogy with this verse as The Method within is a way of Spirit preparing a place for your counsel with God.

I now find myself somewhat free of worry. I am calm and form my own opinions. I am an author, host and radio show personality, a coach and a speaker. If it were not for this filter, I would not have owned the validity of my voice and transformed in the way I have. To quote an old school friend *'the ugly duckling has turned into a swan'*.

It is my mission to pay this Method forward en masse, to stop the cycle of self-sabotage so that we can all be the difference to our generation and beyond. I want us to stand firm in who we are and be strong enough to not care what other people think. Be strong enough to not buy into other people's opinion and feel empowered to express our authentic voice for the betterment of our society.

This book will serve to once and for all strip you of the programming of others and free you from adopting perspectives that stand in the way of Truth. It's time to own your uniqueness and discover the freedom to **be the difference.**

'When you are immune to the opinions of others, you will avoid being the victim of mindless suffering.' (Don Miguel Ruiz)

VALERIE A. CAMPBELL

VALERIE A. CAMPBELL

Find Your Inner Voice

The Enigma

1. The Question

When I came to, I realised I'd been doodling again...

As I sat at my office desk with a pen in hand, twirling it to and fro, the flurry of thread orders now calm, I could feel the warmth of the summer's breeze against my heated skin as it swooped in for a kiss, soft and gentle against my neck.

It's a beautiful summer day, the exit doors are open and I long to be outside in the glorious sunshine instead of stuck in this little back street office somewhere in the East End of London, working within the shaded confines of its entity.

A significant part of my job is to match the exact thread colour to the swatches of material brought in by clients of the rag trade, whose business it is to make and sell clothes, especially women's.

I feel so lethargic, my limbs are languid and I'm a little dozy, no doubt from the heat outside and I ask myself once again, is there more?

You see, I'd been offered this job twice. My old area manager from the previous thread company I'd worked for had served me redundancy and on leaving he'd said: 'I've got a new job for you which is right up your street!' I remember thinking, how could you possibly know what's up my street? You have no idea as to my aspirations; such was my internal rhetoric at the time.

And how could he? I was an introverted young woman in my early 20s who didn't voice my opinions, much less my aspirations; however, he could see I was competent and a quick learner.

I'd initially refused the role but due to no other offers, I'd accepted and found that I actually enjoyed the job. I was the perfect fit, albeit for a salary well below my par, yet I was grateful. I especially liked that customers would ask specifically for me. I felt valued. 'I want only to speak to Valerie', they would say in their Mediterranean accent. You see, I have a gift which had been brought to my attention through formal testing in one of their labs. I possess 100% colour vision which explained my ability to match thread colours exactly to clients' swatches of material.

Brrrr!! The sudden buzzing of the phone jerked me out of my reverie; and as I was beckoned hastily by its urgent flashing green light, I pulled forward my note pad, pen poised, ready to take the order.

'PEM Thread, Valerie speaking'. I took the order and deftly slipped it into the tray for the warehouse to assemble and slumped back in my chair, waiting for the next call, simultaneously glancing down at the large office pad in front of me.

There, something arrested my attention.

As I leant forward, I couldn't help but notice the words I must have written whilst in my mode of reflection, staring hard back up at me, stark in black ink against the white of the page.

To know the difference between right and wrong

I look at the words and feel confused, I'm puzzled... it's not the first time I've written these words. What does it mean? How long will this enigma haunt me...?

You see... I don't know... Is it a question? There is no question mark...

Or is it an answer to something I need to know?

I scratch my head and at the same time feel the confusion spread over my face till it nestles as a furrow between my brows... I need clarity.

Do I not know the difference between right and wrong...? I do, don't I? ... What is the difference?

The phone rang again, and again immediately distracted I reach for the phone, but not before glancing once more at the words as I ask myself, 'will I ever understand its meaning?'

WISDOM KEY
It's the questions that drive us

---

2. The Answer

The years have passed, it's 1996, I'm in my mid-20s and there have been many instances where those words have downloaded through me onto paper; and just as fleetingly, I brush away; like cobwebs that enshroud my vision. I comfort myself that one day the enigma will be resolved.

It's another day at the office. Except this time, I no longer work in the rag trade; it is now environmental services, and I am the only female in an otherwise all-male environment. There are easily over 100 men and I love it!

I was doing some paperwork, having sent my 'boys', as I fondly call them, out to clear the refuse and overflowing bins. It was Friday at about 6 pm and I was looking forward to attending a seminar after work as it was led by a leading personal development coach whose work I respected.

I'd developed an insatiable appetite for anything to do with my self-growth and spiritual development. I was not only into personal development as it was taught in the secular world but also how it was taught through the word of God. My Christian faith was and is very important to me. It was no surprise then, that while for some on a Friday night, it was cinema tickets and popcorn; for me, it was seminar tickets and a notepad!

I was momentarily distracted as one of the lads dumped his bag and clipboard on the counter. As I responded to his 'have a great weekend', I bent my head to attend to my admin and clearly, without being aware, I must have drifted off, as once again, there were the words...

To know the difference between right and wrong

Hmmm, I wondered as I tapped my ballpoint pen, in staccato fashion against the letters; 'What do I need to learn?' The phrase, the statement, I didn't know what to call it, dripped more frequently now from my pen, like the final sands in an hourglass, ready to have its final hour.

It was time to go. I grabbed my handbag, shouted a quick goodbye to my colleague and headed to my car. I'd have to park and jump on the Tube to get to my destination - something I wasn't looking forward to – rush hour in central London is no joke!

Minutes later, as I stood on the train, pressed to others like sardines in a tin and at the peril of unpleasant odours with only the intermittent reprieve of the opening and closing of the carriage doors, I acknowledged I'd done a lot of self-growth recently and I wasn't ready to come off that train just yet, if ever.

I felt like I was on a journey to somewhere - unaware of my destination. I'd had a troubled childhood and had come to the realisation I had a choice on how I show up in this life. I toyed with the book in my hands, 'Acts of Faith, by Iyanla Vanzant; the contents of which were medicine to my soul. My self-esteem had crept up over the years, I was no way as shy as I used to be, yet still far from where I aspired to be...

The carriage eventually stopped at Victoria Station and spat me out on to the platform with the other sardines. Through the tunnel, I travelled, up the escalators before bursting out of the underground, onto the pavement.

I walked the short few minutes to the Millennium Hotel at Victoria and as I passed through the hotel's revolving doors, I saw the seminar advertising banner, pointing in the direction I should go. I took the lift to the floor I needed and then gingerly stepped through the seminar room door.

The room is quiet and still.

I make out that there are approximately 30 people in the room, sitting cross-legged on the heavily patterned carpet. There's a guy sat on the stage, he must be the coach and he's speaking in a soft, melodic and admittedly annoyingly, slow voice.

My heart's still pounding from the journey and as I lower myself to the floor, I can hear my inner voice loud in the stillness of the room, 'Is this guy for real? Is this what you've come for? I hope he starts soon. This is boring.' And as I sat there with the attendees, I began to feel the slowing down of my pounding heart to the pace of the Coach's voice and I realise he's being deliberate.

He was guiding us to a place of stillness - bearing in mind we'd all just come in from our busy environments and he needed us all on the same page. My inner voice became calm and I soon began to appreciate the Coach's soothing words. I began to feel very relaxed. 'I think I'm going to enjoy this.'

My weekend has begun.

It's the next day and I've had a thoroughly inspirational and thought-provoking morning. Andy, the Coach, announced a break and as the attendees flurried out, I made my way to the front of the room to ask him a question.

Andy was speaking to one of the other attendees so I decided to wait patiently until it was my turn. The room was set up seminar style with chairs to the left and chairs to the right with an aisle that ran along the middle. As I took a seat to the right, my eyes roamed the room appraisingly... I felt liberated, light, ethereal almost, with a centred-ness I cannot quite describe.

As I sat there gently tapping my feet, I **suddenly** had the most extraordinary experience... I heard a voice... a crystal clear, loud voice, however not from a person, as I sat by myself but from within and yet without... as if it coming from my chest, all around me and yet not... it was as if time momentarily suspended and the voice pronounced with clear simplicity and authority...

"THERE IS NO DIFFERENCE"

I was startled into tears that gushed instantaneously. The tears of astonishment were of sheer joy, intense gratitude for the relief of knowing. Knowing this was **The Answer** to the words that had held me in its clutches all those years. I felt free!

Refreshing, light, feeling cleansed somehow, I basked in it! I recall the singularity of that moment, a moment so profound that it left me in a head-spin, never to be forgotten... an imprint forever sealed on the consciousness of my mind.

I *knew* what I'd heard was TRUTH... I couldn't explain how I knew this. I just did.

INSTANTLY my all-too-familiar voice kicked in, the one I recognised, this time though, feeling somewhat insidious, seemingly logical.

'What do you mean there is no difference between right and wrong? **Everyone knows** there's a difference between right and wrong' *Where had I heard that tone before? It felt familiar...*

Andy the Coach looked across at me, at my face awash with tears. I imagine I had a stunned look on my face; after all, I had just experienced, what was, for me, an epiphany - a profound insight. I remember walking over towards him and babbling about what had just happened and all the while Andy just slowly nodded his head.

As I glided out of the room, held in the light of that rapturous moment, I asked myself, 'Had the answer always been there? Had the Voice just needed me still enough to hear it?' I truly believe this was a divine appointment. That truth would now replace the grip of its predecessor and would now serve as a filter through which I saw and interacted with everyone around me.

For many years I sought to make sense of it. An enigma replaced by an enigma. A puzzle still to be solved, I revealed only to a few people, for fear they'd think me a few sandwiches short of a picnic basket; as we say in the East End - besides, how could I explain something I didn't even understand? Something I couldn't articulate even to myself? I needed time to make sense of it before I even considered further sharing it... but once I'd made sense of it, what was I to do with it?

It reminded me of a hypothesis experiment I'd done at school; you assume a thing to be true and then seek to prove it, to make sense of it.

Except this wasn't an assumption, this was a *knowing*... and so I shut it away, or so I thought I did; unknowing that it had a grip of me, manoeuvring me like a puppet, from its subconscious confines, as it grew within the receptacle of my mind.

I had always thought that on receiving the answer, the enigma would be solved. Little did I know that it was only the beginning! As my level of questions grew over time, so did my understanding.

So what did I come to understand? Well, it's time for me to share this with you. After all, what is the point of knowledge, if not to be shared?

You should know I am not a scientist or a highfalutin scholar, but what I am, is a person of sound mind - a person of reason and increasing spiritual awareness. I imagine you may be too and so it is my mission to share with you spiritual insights and stories that have pulled my understanding together.

From henceforth I shall refer to 'No Difference Between Right and Wrong' as **'The NDBRW Method'** as it has given way to many approaches to a freer life.

This is a very powerful and profound book please do not take the methods in this lightly.

Let's begin.

WISDOM KEY

Answers come from the most unexpected of places

Different Perspectives

The Enigma Unfolds

3. The New Lens: 'The NDBRW Method'

The messages that shape us

As I share my insights and stories throughout this book, I want you to bear in mind that my personal experience is simply that - *my personal experience.* I say this because it's not a question of whether it is *right or wrong,* it is my perspective based on the content within the glass of my mind.

This means you don't have to buy into my view or even believe a word I say. The importance of which will unveil itself as we dive deeper into our journey.

I was gifted The NDBRW Method via the voice of God's spirit, which I believe lives in every one of us. We are spiritual beings, and I believe we have physical ears to hear because we first heard spiritually... and we still can, if we want to.

And I say 'gifted', because with one fell swoop, a whole set of beliefs which had previously limited my potential, fell away from me. Like a giant wrecking ball to the walls, I had inadvertently built around me, and as the walls fell slowly, softly... I began to feel free.

I remember many years later, jack-knifing out of my sleep to The Voice; again, loud and authoritative 'How can I change you with walls all around you!?'

I saw a vision of four lines of rubble that formed a square, the remains of which looked like a broken- down tower and I took comfort in the thought, 'Well at least the walls are broken down...'

I now recognise this as a premonition of what was to be - not just for me - but for you as the lead-up to the writing of this book.

Dear reader, I intend that The NDBRW Method serves as an opportunity for you to be freed. A release from strongholds that have you shackled to false teachings of who you are, the lies that separate you from *the truth*, which we will go into, in more depth as we travel along.

At this point in our journey I want you, as an analogy, to imagine your mind as a glass vessel. I want you to know that you **are not** what's in the glass - you are the glass. The glass contains your programming, your values and your conditioning from this world, which forms your perception of who you *think* you are.

Who do you think is pouring in and influencing the content within your glass? Think, parents, TV, media, music, teachers, politicians, religion, culture etc.

In the same way, you are not your arms or your legs, you are not your mind. You have a body and you have a mind. They are just part of you. You are a spiritual being... and when you step back from being the voice of your worldly programming and become the voice of who you truly are, then you will have found the key to true freedom.

I believe that seminar weekend allowed me to press pause on the programs that played in the glass of my mind, allowing me to *finally* hear the whisper of The Voice that I believe wants to reset and restore us to our original self.

Now, reader, in terms of my reset; the first teaching/healing I received from The Voice's message was on *judgement*; the lesson was, that it was the *programme* I played internally that gave rise to how I judged others and how I was by no means fit or otherwise competent to judge, based on my narrow and false perspective.

The only One competent to judge perfectly is The Voice of God which lies in His sole ability to see OVER ALL perspectives, therefore what He declares is Truth.

I want us to now look at our understanding of 'seeing the whole picture' versus our understanding of a perspective. I illustrate this by sharing the following insights.

INSIGHT 1 - The Tree

'No two men see the same tree the same way'.

Over the years I had become sensitive to The Voice and its presence. Along the journey, I had learnt to be still, open and expectant of the voice that I now simply refer to as 'Spirit'.

It was not uncommon for me to have a conversation with Spirit whilst washing the dishes in the morning, whilst my mind was still, allowing the water to gently flow, slow over the circular motion of my hands... feeling as one.

Sometimes we would talk on a walk in the nearby park or on a journey to the gym, on the train, in the car; I felt always connected... just a conversation away. Our relationship deepened over the years. Spirit had become my friend, teacher and confidante. I sought out Spirit's direction regularly.

This particular day, Spirit taught me a lesson. One day as I sat at my desk quietly working from home, Spirit's voice alerted me to the tree that stood outside my window.

Spirit: 'Do you see that tree?'

Me: 'Yes,' I replied, to the voice I now easily recognised.

Spirit: 'If you were sat on that bench beneath the tree and were to look up at that tree, you would be adamant it is above you?'

Me: 'Yes', I replied, wondering where this was going...

Spirit: 'And yet...if you were on that aeroplane, you see flying above, you would be adamant that tree is below you?'

Me: 'Yes, of course' I replied... now getting an inkling of where this was going.

Spirit: 'Which version of you is right?' said Spirit.

Me: 'Well depending from where you view it, both' I replied.

Spirit: 'And which wrong?'

Me: 'Well depending from where you view it, both,' I replied yet again.

Spirit: 'At the same time.' Pronounced Spirit.

'You see, your answer is the same. You are both right and both wrong at the same time, there is no difference. The only difference is from where you stand. Literally, your point of view and so it is the world over.

'Tell me, how many arguments have you witnessed where one tries to impress their 'right' upon another? Is this not how your wars are created...?'

I thought about what Spirit had taught me that day...

"my people perish for the lack of knowledge." (Hosea 4:6) came to mind...

I was both right and wrong at the same time. When one has an argument I could see that it is simply a clash of perspectives not *knowledge* AND how nonsensical it is to argue and engage in conflict.

How nonsensical would it be then to judge one over the other when they are both wrong and yet right, both at the same time?

Spirit had shown me that:

When all you see is conflict, you lose sight of peace, whilst peace waits patiently at your side, awaiting recognition. Your engagement in conflict is merely a distraction from peace. You do not have answers...you have points of view.

Reader, can you see why we need not buy into another's judgement, or point of view and disregard our own; in effect, abandon ourselves to follow the path of another or a path that is not our own?

INSIGHT 2 - The Zoom

'We make sense of a world based on an incomplete picture...'

Your right is their wrong and their right is your wrong. Why? Because, from both your points of view, neither of you will ever have full knowledge of the whole picture. They will only ever see part of the picture as will you... therefore, it is written that you should *'not lean on your own understanding'* (Proverbs 3:5-6)

Case in point...

One day, whilst watching TV from the sofa, I saw something that brought a further unfolding of the enigma.

On the screen I saw a woman with a handbag over her shoulder walking along a pavement, minding her own business. All of a sudden, a guy, as if from nowhere, rushed at her and shoved her to the ground with such force the contents of her bag scattered!

Indignantly I jumped up from my seat with thoughts of WTF! (excuse my French), thinking 'This is the problem these days, how is it a woman can't walk down the road in peace with scum like this on the street... that's what makes the world...' such was my internal rant.

It took me a minute to notice, as the camera slowly zoomed out, a bigger picture and what I saw forced me to slowly slump back in my chair with a feeling of being chastised.

You see, as the camera panned out, it revealed she was walking alongside a scaffolded building and precariously positioned, loose bricks were about to fall... it was the 'offender's' intention to save her life!

I realised we make snap judgements on people's motives all the time. We even make judgements on people we've never met as if we know them. We judge on the colour of their skin, body shape, attire, creed, height, status - the list goes on. We do this without seeing the full picture and we congratulate ourselves on our false judgements; it's laughable!

At that very moment I thought, how many times have we borne witness to a situation where what we judged to be 'wrong', then became 'right' when we saw a fuller picture?

Dear reader, how many instances can you recall where you have changed your opinion? Too many to count on both hands and feet, I imagine!

There are billions of people judging from within the windows of their glass mind, creating a matrix of conflict all over the world.

From where God is standing, your wrong and your right equate to the same, as it's based on a small slice of His view which is ubiquitous! You cannot see the whole picture as He can.

INSIGHT 3 - The House of Colours

'To not see the whole is to not see the truth.'

My experience has taught me that to understand, we often need to hear something said in a different way for it to be understood. I came across the extract below on the internet and it perfectly encapsulated this teaching on The NDBRW Method.

Whilst reading the section below, imagine the opening line is from a gentleman, questioning a lady. For this analogy, I am in appreciation to the author - Megan Chance.

****

"'Imagine you come upon a house painted brown. What colour would you say the house was?"

"Why brown, of course."

"But what if I came upon it from the other side, and found it to be white?"

"That would be absurd. Who would paint a house two colours?"

He ignored my question. "You say it's brown, and I say it's white. Who's right?"

"We're both right."

"No," he said. "We're both wrong. The house isn't brown or white. It's both. You and I only see one side. But that doesn't mean the other side doesn't exist. To not see the whole is to not see the truth."

****

Did you have to read that several times, to understand the author's perspective? Always seek first to understand; so let us continue in this vein... It's no different than if I showed you the palm of my hand; you cannot see the back of my hand because your senses will not allow you to see it. We only ever see one side at a time. To not see the other side doesn't mean it doesn't exist.

Therefore, to not see the whole is to see an illusion – a falsehood *founded on a mistaken impression;* or we may say, to not see the truth is to buy into a false reality. We must be aware that there are possibilities that exist outside of our perspective.

Learning Points

1. Human Beings – Perspective:

In "The Lesson of the Tree" you are introduced to different perspectives.

The Lesson reveals you can be both right and wrong at the same time - there is no difference. The only difference is your perspective - your point of view.

2. God – Vision (Overall perspective)

In the Lesson of the Zoom, you are introduced to God's OVERALL perspective.

The key learning here is God is both the 'right' and the 'wrong' at the same time. There is no difference.

Why? Because of His ubiquitous nature - He is everywhere at the same time. He has no opposite, for there he is also... even in your past, present and future.

3. Perspective Vs Vision:

a.   The House of Colours illustrates that God is an-all-inclusive God - He includes brown and white.

b.   We also see through the Zoom story the potential negative impact it can have when we judge based on our perspective, rather than depending on God's knowledge, which is based on his complete vision – His overall perspective. This demonstrates the logic in standing on His word.

c.   Appearances can change, depending on where you're looking from, which means that it is an illusion. But what is real is changeless.

This whole book is about you buying into God's viewpoint, his truth. I pray that in the depositing of this one seed, The NDBRW Method, that many eyes will begin to open.

WISDOM KEY

You do not have the answer, you have points of view

Release Limiting Perspectives

4. The Reasoning Exercise

'Love your neighbour, as you love yourself' (Mark 12:31)

Taking time to reflect on my epiphany and listening to Spirit, I asked myself; what were the effects of this message? How had it changed me? What fruits had it borne? What direction had it forced me to go?

As I answer these questions, I invite you to **join me** on an exercise below, please ponder on these answers with me. My aim here is to demonstrate how The NDBRW Method changed my perspective and how it may affect yours.

> *Tell me;* **if you believed there to be no difference between right and wrong indicate which of the following statements would ring true for you?**

I have shared the answers that rang true for me; you may or may not agree with my answers and that's ok, as God knows the mind in which this seed is deposited and the timing of its fruition.

Let us begin: When I believe there to be **No difference** between right and wrong...

STATEMENT	True	False
I felt as if I wasn't being judged as 'wrong' by God		
I felt equal to another i.e. 'no-one is better than me'		
I felt no need to compare – I run my own race		
I felt satisfied and whole in my uniqueness		
I felt somehow liberated – free to be me!		
I seriously curbed my judging of another		
I reined in my negative self-talk		
I dissolved feelings of regret		
Mind-set wise, I felt I'd been 'reset' - given a level playing field		
I refused to engage in arguments		
I agreed to disagree, with peace, on another's opinion		
I felt no need to prove or justify myself to another		
I felt humble		
I felt unjustified to *not* forgive		
I lost the need to make excuses for myself		
I respected my opinion as much as anyone else's		
I felt strong self-acceptance and of others		
I felt peaceful - at one with myself		
I felt confident in myself, since I didn't need validation from another or seek out their approval		
I felt confident irrespective of another's education or background		
I no longer felt intimidated by anyone		
I acquired this feeling of boldness		
I felt free from fear to voice my opinion		
I felt that my opinion was just as valid as another		
I felt that I was my only competition		

	True	False
I felt no need to war with others		
I felt no need to attack		
I felt no need to impose my beliefs on others or have them impose theirs on me		
I felt free of the need to control others		
I felt free to be authentic and not wear a mask		
I felt it ok to be truly seen by others		
I felt in integrity with myself – in alignment		
I felt inclined to see the good in others		
I felt oneness with who I met *not* 'separate'		
I was able to quickly establish rapport; as I listened to others from a place of non-judgement, they felt a level of trust and comfort in opening up to me		
I felt love for me		
I felt worthy of love		
I felt enough		

Dear Reader, can you feel the reset I gained to protect the integrity of who I really am? I could feel how this message had brought out an improved version of me. It was by no means something that I observed overnight and it took time for this seed to take root and bear these fruit.

I then **contrasted** it with the world view, as it currently stands - *there is a difference* between right and wrong and how it affected my interaction with others.

> From the filter of this belief, let's explore whether the statements resonate as **true or false for you?**

Let's take a look and see whether the world view, by contrast, makes you a better you. Again, indicate your view with a tick in the True/False box.

When I believed **there to be a difference** between right and wrong this is how I felt...

STATEMENT	True	False
I felt as if I was constantly being judged		
I felt unequal to another		
I felt 'divided' within		
I felt somehow shackled – not free		
I didn't appreciate my uniqueness		
I felt it normal to judge another and them me		
I was hard on myself in terms of negative self-talk		
I felt justified to hold onto regrets		
Mind-set wise, I felt disadvantaged		
I would engage in arguments		
I felt it ok to war with others to get my point across		
I'd not necessarily disagree with peace on another's' opinion		
I felt a need to constantly prove or justify myself		
I felt superior to some and inferior to others		
I felt there were many reasons to not forgive		
I felt it necessary to make excuses for myself		
I did not respect my opinion as much as anyone else's		
I didn't feel in full acceptance of myself or indeed others		
I felt conflict - a lack of peace within		
I lacked confidence in myself, I felt a need to be validated by others and sought out their approval		
I felt smaller by another's higher education, title or more strongly expressed opinion		
I could be intimidated		
I was shy - boldness was a far reach for me		

	True	False
I felt timid and anxious to voice my opinion		
I felt that my opinion held no validity		
I constantly self-guessed, self-edited what I wished to say and so never *truly* listened		
I felt I was competing with others to excel - comparing		
I felt a need to attack to protect my 'corner'		
I felt a need to impose my beliefs on others or have them impose theirs on me		
I felt a need to control others		

So what was the impact?

My feelings changed because my thoughts changed. My self-BELIEFS changed because of this NDBRW seed. How I felt impacted my life since my actions – my interactions got that much more peaceful.

You see, conflict comes from the energy of 'I'm right and you're wrong; it's divisive energy that causes separation - pain; and we see it in conversations around relationships, politics and religion.

When you feel 'wrong' around a person it dismantles trust. It stops you from trusting the person to 'hear' or to respect you. How we communicate about subjects such as religion and politics or issues in relationships doesn't have to be divisive when you practice suspending judgement.

Looking at life through the filter of The NDBRW Method allowed me to suspend judgement, therefore positively changed my energy in how I interact with others, and as I began to walk in that elevated energy, I essentially became what I felt.

The NDBRW Method will allow you to have a mind that is both open and unattached. It will cause you to exercise self-control; an ability to exercise self-restraint. I am often told I exude a sense of calm and am not quick to anger.

Dear Reader, it's important to note that you don't know you're attached or living in a falsehood until you *suspend yourself* and observe it from a place devoid of judgement. The 'Answer', my epiphany, allowed me to become a fish out of water. The lies we swim in give rise to a false reality.

I believe God gave me the realisation of NDBRW so that my mind could *become like a baby again, not knowing the difference between right and wrong* – 'soil' for the impact of His word to take root and like a bud of a plant, open in perfect time... so that eventually, I, in turn, can plant this seed in yours.

Will you allow it to take root in your mind today? Your choice.

Remember, I am not here to judge if your perspective is right or wrong. I'm acknowledging it's just that - your perspective; and your perspective - your judgements, creates your reality. Are you happy with your reality? If not, *know* that you have the power to change it.

Often in the summertime, I'm asked when at home, 'Why do you leave your front door open? Are you crazy? Aren't you afraid you'll attract thieves and robbers?'

My answer is 'No'. Why 'No'? Because that is their perspective, not mine. I choose to not buy into it. My perspective is the opposite and as such, I have not attracted thieves and robbers. I have, on a few occasions, forgotten to lock the front door, gone to the supermarket and returned home to find my home intact. No cops or robbers! Your beliefs always seek to be actualised.

Living life the NDBRW Method has allowed me to say 'No'.

I say NO to a reality that does not serve me and say YES to one that does. I say NO to people-pleasing.

We need to learn to wield the power of NO. NO can save you time. NO can save you money. NO can save you resources. NO can save your sanity. NO can protect your love life. NO can save your sexual health. NO can maintain your boundaries, therefore No will preserve your integrity. NO is a powerful word that we can use with assertion.

It's time to stand up for your true self and run your unique race.
'...and let us run with perseverance the race marked out for us'
(Hebrews 12:1)

WISDOM KEY
It's in the relinquishment of judgement that you find yourself

5. The Equation of God's Outcome

Anything of equal value is the same in God's eyes

One day on a whim of inspiration, as directed by the Spirit, I wrote NDBRW as a mathematical equation. I had been looking up the synonyms for the phrase 'no difference' and saw words such as 'oneness', 'unity', 'same', 'identical' and 'of equal value' and so I wrote **'no difference between right and wrong'** NDBRW as an equation:

Right – Wrong = Zero

Looking at the equation, I could see that for the outcome to equal zero; right and wrong would have to be of the same value.

Another way to interpret this is to replace the word 'difference' with the synonym word 'inequality' - Therefore, 'There is no inequality between right and wrong'.

On observing right or wrong as having no value higher than the other I felt compelled to dig deeper and so I asked Spirit... why do you see them as having the same value? Gently, Spirit replied, because *they make no difference to my outcome...whatever I call it, it will become.*

Like a child, God feeds us with morsels we can handle; always there is more when we are ready to receive.

I meditated on this answer; I knew there was something more for me to understand... What was I not seeing, in the way that He sees? In what way was my interpretation, my perspective not aligned with His? What I had learnt, *thus far* when I observed the effect it had on my interaction with others, had begun to make sense *experientially*... however, I sensed there was more.

The message was now in my glass blossoming and colouring my perspective. I could feel a direction in the turn of its branches. I had noticed that when speaking with others, no matter their station in life, I would think, 'Your opinion is just as valid as mine.'

In levelling the playing field, it caused me to have a strong sense of self-validation and not necessarily buy into another's opinion, no matter how strongly they expressed it unless it served me.

As if a reset button had been pressed, I did not allow myself to feel pressured or to waiver over what I believed. My new filter reminded me that my opinion mattered - therefore my confidence increased, my emotional intelligence increased and dare I say it... I began to believe in my Voice.

It had taken years of much self-exploration to understand why there was no difference between right and wrong. I thought I'd fully solved it - that I shouldn't get caught up with the perspective of others... right?

However, there was a second lesson... the branches had turned to a new phase of learning.

Whilst I had been focused on the left part of the equation, i.e. the learning around perspectives, Spirit showed me that God's focus was on the right - **His outcome.**

Whilst we squabble amongst ourselves as to what is right and wrong, God is saying my outcome remains the same – to me there is no difference.

He was showing me, right or wrong makes no difference to Him. He showed me I should not worry or hold onto any past mistakes because once I placed my trust in him, He would use my mistakes to refine and re-direct me for that which he had pre-purposed.

For we are God's masterpiece. He has created us anew in Christ Jesus, so we can do the good things he planned for us long ago. (Ephesians 2:10) - New Living Translation **(NLT)**

The journey I had made in my effort to solve the enigma, was what God had designed for my *undoing* to prepare me for the work he had placed in me and what he had planned, required me to be bold.

Today people readily recognise this trait in me. They say 'you have this boldness about you.' When you know the truth, it is inevitable. I am no longer a shy little thing, I have renewed my identity.

God's word tells us:

'And we know that all things work together for good to those who love God, to those who are the called according to His purpose.' (Romans 8:28)

Today, at the time of writing I heard an affirmative word from the actor, writer and producer, Tyler Perry as he spoke at the 25th Essence Festival, New Orleans.

When he was asked, 'What was the greatest mistake you made?

He responded with: *"I haven't made any mistakes... I'll tell you why. Everything I thought was a mistake God turned around and worked that thing out for my good. He joined the dots and I saw that if I hadn't done that, then that wouldn't have worked and then I wouldn't have met that person and that wouldn't have worked... you have to get into the flow of God and just surrender..."*

Look at what Tyler Perry has achieved today! A 330-acre movie-making studio in Atlanta - God is always focused on the outcome.

Oprah Winfrey says: *'Learn from every mistake, because every experience, encounter and particularly your mistakes, are there to teach you and force you into being more of who you are.'*

The Bible tells us:

'In him we were also chosen, having been predestined according to the plan of him who works out everything in conformity with the purpose of his will' (Ephesians 1:11)

God knows us, he knows our ways and has factored in deviations from our path. By its very nature, a plan doesn't necessarily go the way we want it to. What plan is infallible? What plan works out as perfectly as intended? By its very definition, a plan requires 'conformity' to be achieved, but His outcome is the same!

The Bible tells us *'he has made our crooked paths straight'* (Isaiah 45:2) He knows. God knows the outcome. He is the perfect navigator to your destination. 'There is no 'wrong way' because once you allow his voice to direct you, you will get there in perfect time. You will finish your race as He stands at your destination.

Dear reader, as you move through your journey, you have to understand that there is a world of infinite possibilities that lie outside of your perspective, but often we're too scared to step out of our comfort zone to get to the destination for which we have been preordained. Why? **Because we fear what we cannot control.**

We depend on our naked eye and our physical senses, knowing deep down this is not enough and because we think we're not enough, it's easy for us to sway and lean into someone else's perspective. However, cradled in the loving arms of God, where we were always meant to be, we are enough.

God gives us time and he gives us His voice. Will you allow the sands of time to run out before arriving at your destination, because of fear? Your faith is the answer.

I remember in 2005 nose-diving out of a job I had in North London, with nothing to land on except faith. I had no backup plan. It was scary but I felt the fear and did it anyway.[1]

I remember almost losing my home. I had accrued arrears as I had no income to pay the mortgage and at the eleventh hour,

God showed up for me through a friend, blessing me in part with the outstanding amount that I owed. There have been so many instances of 'just in time' throughout my life. Why? Because I trusted in The Voice and I listened.

Remember: Jesus said, *'Whoever has ears to hear, let them hear'* (Mark 4:9.)

For those familiar with the TV series, Prison Break; the main character, Michael Schofield, always kept his eye on the desired outcome. He never once swayed from it, despite the 'wrong' stuff that happened along the way, he used it as paving stones to correct the path to meet his ultimate destination - a prison break.

I pray that you too will experience a prison break, from the judgements that shackle you!

WISDOM KEY
You are not a slave, time to undo those shackles

---

1. Feel the Fear and Do It Anyway, *Susan Jeffers, Vermillion 2007*

6. The Birthplace of Illusions

The source of our separation

Where did this belief stem from - that there is a difference between right and wrong? I believe it to be the fruit of 'we are not enough'... but then from where did this lie that we are not enough come from? Well...let me share my thoughts with you.

You may be familiar with the story of Adam and Eve. Whether you believe it to be an actual story or a metaphor, we witness for the first time, the indoctrination of a thought, a lie that is contrary to the will of God.

We see how Eve follows through on a *suggestion* made by the Devil in the form of a serpent, that she is less than what God says she is - that she is not enough, and as he plants this seed of doubt within her, it grows branches of imperfection, inadequacy, and vulnerability. A new belief takes hold and inevitably gives rise to her biting into *the fruit* of separation.

Now, why do I say separation? Because God had already warned, in the eating of this fruit, they would surely die; and so in her eating of it, Eve's will ceased to be at one with the will of God; and to separate from that which gives life is death. It's not dissimilar to a patient that is disconnected from a life-support machine.

Difference came into play the moment Eve's will was no longer in agreement with God's will. God and his sons and daughters in union with him do not think differently. The concept of right and wrong did not exist. It was just one will.

We then see how the fruit bore more separation when Adam also bit into it. We see how the fall-out of separation has been passed down from generation to generation. *It is our perceived separation that is the cause of pain...* and the only thing that changed was **perception... perspective.**

They no longer saw themselves as innocent and in the belief that they were somehow blemished and needed to be well or made whole, they bit into the fruit to satisfy the **illusion** that they were less than perfect i.e., not enough.

A fruit will only bear fruit of its kind, of its own likeness. Lies breed more lies. Illusions breed more illusions. Anything outside of the truth is merely that, an illusion! It is not real.

Our perceived rights and our perceived wrongs outside of The Truth equates to the same. Neither is of greater value in the world of illusions...

We live in this world of our own making, not the life that was written for us.

Through this account, we can see how our beliefs give rise to feelings which give rise to actions thus our results. What illusions have you bitten into? What lies have you swallowed ... just like Eve... and Adam?

Today, we see political tactics... agendas... and we bite into the illusion of it, and often in the form of mass hysteria we walk in it... but is it really so?

The time is NOW to break hold of beliefs that imprison you from knowing the true life; to break free from the self-imposed judgements that disable you from reaching your true potential. That place, that you secretly long for, is found in a restored and renewed mind. It is in this state that you will see you were never separate from God.

WISDOM KEY
The source of our pain is in our separation

---

7. Back to Innocence

Clothed with 'His' covering

After eating the fruit, Adam and Eve hid their nakedness from God; hiding, what they now saw as tarnished, their innocence. Before this, they never felt the necessity to cover their nakedness.

I imagine a fish when separated from water – it's covering; feels isolated, naked, vulnerable and exposed. God never wanted this for you, there-fore he wants you stripped of these lies. He wants you bare, to receive His covering of righteousness and for you to recognise you are one with Him.

When you recognise you are one with God you do not feel 'exposed'. You feel 'covered'. Today, as part of your restoration, God wants you vulnerable and open to him, to receive all that he has in store for you.

The NDBRW Method's stance on evil

It may have occurred to you, it certainly did to me, what then does NDBRW mean in terms of evil?

Well, as long as there is an opposing will opposite to the infinite wisdom of God, then evil will continue in this world. Evil stems from the lies that would bring harm and moral wickedness to your brother or your sister.

God doesn't stop a lot of things that cause Him pain, it's the price of FREE will, knowing that everything bears consequences, no matter how painful they are. We reap what we sow; and if we choose to buy into evil, the outcome is destruction.

You see, the serpent is never at rest and is ferociously up to its deception, sowing seeds of discord and disunity that give rise to illusions that exist in our minds which are extended through our isolation and separation, just like the serpent did to Eve.

Throughout time we see the perpetuation of wars, slavery, murder, rape, family, relationship, mental and physical health breakdowns, unspeakable evils - the list continues.

One of its biggest tools for separation in this modern day is Artificial Intelligence (AI) – namely mobile phones. Texting and social media have become all-consuming for both young and old, held captive by the imagery of illusions.

Reader, have you noticed people don't even look at each other anymore? Think family meals, bus stops, trains? AI was intentioned for us connect but it has also served to isolate and separate... think again!

Spiritual warfare is real and there is a drive to keep up the illusion of separation so we can be manipulated in the billions worldwide.

Today, as I currently write in the year 2020, we are faced with a pandemic of catastrophic proportions. Coronavirus (COVID 19) has forced us to further separate and isolate as we deal with its effects behind closed doors. The main question is what will God do with the Serpent's intention?

'For we wrestle not against flesh and blood, but against principalities, against powers, against the rulers of the darkness of this world, against spiritual wickedness in high places'
(Ephesians 6:12)

I know I have nothing to fear because no form of evil can overcome the will of God, nothing can thwart his aim but must conform to it. The Perspective over all perspectives (many of which are being shared over the Internet) he will use for our good!

Don't you see, you planned evil against me but God used those same plans for my good, as you see all around you right now – life for many people (Genesis 50:20) (MSG)

Life for many people since we are now placed in a position to truly appreciate the abundance that we live in; the relationships that we take for granted, our health, our luxuries, our nature, our freedom! God has used what was intended for evil for us to change our perspective; and in our isolation, we can see what is important, our unity, not our separation; and in our connection, we jointly take part to heal our land.

I hope that many will stop attacking God and let go of the idea that *He has separated Himself from us*. That this will make humanity realise that they are part of something much bigger than their perspective and hear what God has always been saying...

'I am the LORD, and there is no other; apart from me there is no God. I will strengthen you, though you have not acknowledged me.' (Isaiah 45:5)

Fortunately, through God's vision, He loves us as He originally sees us; our identity and value to Him remain unchanged. The NDBRW Method will remove the veil from your eyes and assist your return, back to innocence; to the innocence of a child who does not know the difference between right and wrong.

God sees your innocence

God sees you exactly as He created you, you are perfect. However, it is you who do not see yourself that way... and it is you who walk in the imperfection that you are not enough. God doesn't create warped people; you are perfectly packaged for your purpose without blemish.

He did not say you are wonderfully made or that you are a masterpiece or that He created you very well by mistake! *'He is not a man that He should lie.'* (Numbers 23:19) He created you as a whole person with the end in His mind.

What will you choose to believe in - the illusion or the Truth? Either way, your life will unfold as a self-fulfilling prophecy, or a 'God written' fulfilling prophecy. You choose.

Much like the story of the ugly duckling, who never really was a duck, yet felt vulnerable, alone, isolated and not enough and never fitted in *until* it discovered its true identity - it was really a swan!

May you too discover your true identity in God and like the swan, return to its house of innocence.

WISDOM KEY
Time to get to grips with the real 'reality'

8. The Illusion: 'Stolen' Money

In the above chapter we see how not believing we are enough can lead us to buy into another's judgements that lie outside of the true picture. When we do this, we invite ourselves to walk in the insanity of irrational behaviour which will follow suit.

Consider this story.

It was summer 2016 and I was due to travel. A friend had returned a loan of several hundred pounds and I placed the cash in a handbag near the radiator in the kitchen of my home, a place where I keep multiple handbags. I decided to leave the money there with the intention to collect it at the time of my trip.

A month later, a couple of days before travelling, I went to retrieve the money but couldn't find it. I searched the handbag I was certain I had placed it in but it just wasn't there. I carefully searched other handbags beside it, thinking the whole time - where was this money? It was nowhere to be found!

I asked my daughter if she'd seen it, she said she had no idea. At a loss, I shared with my friend who had returned the loan that the money had disappeared. That day he planted a 'seed' in my mind. A suggestion... 'Maybe it was your lodger... who else could it be?'

Isn't it funny how insidious a suggestion can be? Even though I had a belief that 'I only attract good lodgers to me', I'd allowed a seed to be planted and it had unconsciously taken root. The reason I know this, is because it affected my actions. I STOPPED looking for the money and considered it gone... the seed had subtly sunk into the soil within my glass.

Fast forward, approximately a year later:

As I sat on my sofa looking at a list of affirmations I like to read over from time to time, I decided, to focus on the affirmation 'I am a *money magnet*'. I then went to bed with this mantra on my mind, repeating over and over 'I am a money magnet'.

The next morning, I woke with the intention to go to the gym but found myself strangely decluttering. I was in the kitchen clearing paperwork, folding the laundry, sorting my bags - putting some in the hallway cupboard and systematically checking the contents, throwing away old tissues, paraphernalia etc. and just generally putting things in order.

As I approached the kitchen door, I looked at what was hanging behind it. Observing more bags to be decluttered, I pulled at one of the bags, putting my hand in to search its contents and suddenly I paused; for there appeared to be a folded £20-pound note...'ooooh nice!!' I thought as I reached out to claim it!

However, before my hand even touched it, I noticed a curious density to the way it looked and suddenly I realised with a shock, this was the money that had disappeared almost a year ago! I gasped and flopped down on a chair with the bag clasped fast to my chest. Overjoyed at the find and yet quickly reflective...

You see, I realised at that moment that I had bought into another person's perspective - their 'judgement'. I had bitten the fruit and subconsciously, I *had* treated my lodger differently, not in an overt way, yet somehow wary, as I had a question over their character. Whether my lodger picked up on this or not, I cannot say.

However, because I had the filter of The NDBRW Method in my glass, I was able to 'suspend' my behaviour in a way to not damage our relationship. I demonstrated temperance.

Can you relate to this story? How often do we take on the perspectives and judgements of others and follow through on it? Causing havoc and conflict to the innocent around us, because of a suggestion, a misperception, a lie, an illusion!

I went back to thinking about Eve in the Bible. I too had bought into an insidious thought. I too had bitten the fruit. I too had a part of me that felt I wasn't good enough to attract a perfect lodger and so just maybe...

WISDOM KEY
Time to bow out of the opinion of others

Embrace Positive Perspectives

9. The Secret is in the 'I AM'

The I AM is *in* your AIM

In the previous account I referred to 'I am a money magnet'. This is an example of an 'affirmation statement'. It was through the embracing of such statements that I was able to shift my identity.

From my NDBRW experience sprung the belief that I get to choose with freedom, without apology or external validation, the characteristics I wish to show up.

NDBRW gave me a level playing field, the reset button required to see myself on an equal footing with others, i.e. that no-one is more special or less special than I; inspiring me to shift my identity through the power of 'I AM'. The 'I AMs' that you embrace will either increase you or decrease you.

As children we're born into this world, as a clean slate, meaning that our subconscious says 'yes' to everything, to what it's exposed to and doesn't differentiate between right and wrong. Our parents, teachers, influencers are our 'gods' as was God to Adam and Eve.

Therefore what we were told about ourselves created who we **think we are**.

Up until my *awareness*, I had defined myself as 'I Am shy' because I was taught to be quiet. I, therefore, didn't speak up which led to 'I'm awful at public speaking'. I'd second guess myself and my voice would shake. I had learnt to define myself as 'I am worthless' – why then would anyone view my opinion as valid? All of which limited my being-ness.

I had unintentionally cursed myself based on my subconscious programming and kept myself small when I could just as well re-define myself with a set of empowering I AMs which were mine for the choosing.

The NDBRW Method allowed me and will allow you to make those choices as it serves as a bridge. A reset to be as a child again not knowing there to be a difference between right and wrong; a 'pattern interrupt' for you to pause and choose your I AMs.

At one end of the bridge is the old you, the I AMs of yesterday that represent 'who you *think* you are' and at the other end is an opportunity for you to connect with your true identity in who God created you as, with a different set of I AMs that serve you.

"...and learn of Him anew. Now is He born again to you and you are born again to Him" (A Course in Miracles)

(A great movie to watch that demonstrates the power of 'I Am' and the power and impact of creating a new identity is Catch Me

If You Can. It's based on a true story with Leonardo DiCaprio as the protagonist).

So where did 'I AM' come from? **'I AM' is the name of God:**

'And God said unto Moses, I Am That I Am: and he said, Thus shalt thou say unto the children of Israel, I Am hath sent me unto you.' (Exodus 3:14)

Recognition of Your 'I AMs'

When you call on the I AMs that are not part of your conscious reality, you resurrect them from a state of dormancy within you. When you say I Am, you are *recognising* and announcing that part of God within you, to show up and make itself known.

Then all that is around you will conform; will bend to the new concept of yourself, to affirm that what you have chosen to be. It's not dissimilar to the opening up of a kitchen cupboard and reaching for the salt. You believe it to be already there and so you take it because you recognise it.

When I first wrote my I Am statements, some seemed like a long stretch. I Am brave, I Am a boss; it was such a stretch from who I was at that time, it felt like an outright lie. My mind had many examples to the contrary! I felt out of integrity because I wasn't walking my talk.

However, when you believe you are a child of God, it's not so much an affirmation but a recognition. You believe that you are recognising a part of yourself and in so doing you call it forth.

You affirm what you recognise. Now that's a game-changer!

What's amazing is how our mind works. Cognitive dissonance is created when your walk doesn't match your new talk. You experience discomfort and because your mind wants to be right, it will subconsciously change your behaviour to match its new conversation.

You don't just say an affirmation out loud and be done with it - you have to *feel* it. You have to embody it, which means expressing and projecting it out as a vibration to God's universe. Nothing is too much of a stretch for God and I have experienced what I call long and short stretches. Here's an example of what I call a *long stretch.*

In 2018 one of my new affirmations was 'I am an international speaker'. After expressing this with feeling daily, I received a call less than a month later; it was a lady from America, who had interviewed me a few weeks back on my book She's Got That Vibe which explains the Law of Attraction as it relates to dating.

She said: 'Valerie, I have a radio show and I think you'd make a great host of your own. Are you interested?'

It came; seemingly, out of the blue and The Voice within, feeling my doubts, whispered...'You can do it.' I said 'yes' and so I sent the CEO a half-hour pilot show, which was approved and commissioned.

A few months later, after submitting weekly shows to www.bshaniradio.com/the-secret-vibe

I had 250,000 listeners worldwide. It was only then that it dawned on me - I had become an international speaker! My 'I Am' had been recognised, not just by me but by thousands all around the world!

Now let me give you an example of what I perceive as a short stretch. One of my affirmations was 'I am peace'. There was a time I was dating a guy and I'd discovered he was, by his own admission, a pessimist. He had sent me a text message which under normal circumstances I would have responded with anger.

However, because of my internal dialogue, I Am Peace, I looked at the text and with restraint responded in a peaceful way, halting any negativity in its tracks. My mind caused my behaviour to match my new mental conversation. Again, my 'I Am' had been recognised.

Your 'I AMs' Open Doors

Let's look at a few more of my 'I AMs' and how they can unlock your personality and in effect open doors. It's great when you can look back, see the dots, connect them and observe what they unlocked for you.

I Am bold

When I was in my early twenties, I decided to stop being shy. I recognised it didn't serve me and kept me small. I declared inwardly that I needed to be bold and so God presented me with an opportunity to be so.

I had a job interview and I practised mock questions over and over; visualising answering the questions I thought the interviewers would ask me. On the day of the interview, I felt so bold and confident in my answers. Every question I had imagined, they threw at me. Unsurprisingly, I got the job!

Now Reader, remember the mind always wants to be right. The interview caused me to behave in a way to match my new mental conversation 'I Am bold.' *You attract who you are, not what you want* and so the job placed me in an environment which required even more boldness.

My 'I Am bold' wasn't finished with me yet. The post saw me working in Environmental Services alongside more than 100 men, which gave me the perfect platform to exercise confidence and boldness; because let me tell you, you cannot be a wallflower in that environment!

I was the only female in a sea of men and the language that I heard and the dominating male characteristics that I came across, forced me to grow more in both assertiveness and boldness - I had no choice but to be that way in that environment.

In the ten years that I worked there, being bold became an essential part of my personality. At first, it felt uncomfortable but then I got used to it. Working in that environment proved to be an experiential school for me. I had to step up and use both my feminine and masculine energy to get things done and meet deadlines. I loved the way I felt about myself, as the most important relationship you will ever have is the one you have with yourself.

The point I'm making here is, you attract circumstances and you attract people in your life based on your I AMs. You attract behaviours towards you based on your I AMs. That's how important this is. Your I Ams opens doors! They are the keys to your Kingdom.

Affirmation – I Am assertive

One of the I Ams that was a spin-off from I Am bold is, I Am assertive.

In the world of networking, when I am approached by a person and they want to connect with me, it helps when they can see a part of them-self in me. 'I Am assertive.'

When a person can see parts of them-self in another person, they can better relate.

So often, when you look at the people you hang around with most, it's because you see a part of yourself in that person or that which you aspire to. You may also see parts of yourself in a person which you do not want to encourage within yourself and so you choose to not have that person around because you don't want that 'I Am' in yourself to be recognised.

I observe 'I Am assertive' in Thomas Shelby in the hit TV series *Peaky Blinders* or Bishop TD Jakes whom I listened to this morning. We see this in their actions. They acted on the *recognition* of this 'I am' perhaps before it became a firm self-belief and as you now know a belief always wants to be actualised.

Dear reader, all you need do is recognise your I Am. Believe it, feel it and be it. To be means to express it. Yes, at first, it may feel uncomfortable but when you see people responding to you in the way that you feel about yourself, trust me you will think 'Wow... I'm really doing this... and the 'I Am' will solidify itself when you see how well it serves you.

Like I Ams attracts like I Ams; I might flirt with a guy and say: 'You're looking sharp today!' I'm therefore stating the I Am that I see. He responds, 'You're looking beautiful today' and I respond, 'Why thank you', because I know I am. This is the matching 'I Am'. I usually respond with a further 'to God be the Glory' because I'm not denying it's to His glory, and then we both laugh because there is common recognition and we can relate! The reason why

I'm explaining this to you in detail is that I want you to understand the *'why'* to your **act as if** of your selected 'I Am' because if you do not understand the psychology behind it, you will fall out of the habit.

So that is how you insert your new 'I Am' beliefs. Understand that whatever you believe, your actions will follow; and because people see that belief in you, they will reflect it and act in a way that matches what they see.

Beliefs are transferable

When you exude 'I Am confident' on stage, people will believe in your confidence, and more than likely believe in what you have to say. They will embrace your words because you have come across as believing in them.

If someone is on stage and they're nervous, you can *feel* their nervousness and this means the audience will not believe that person as readily. You will doubt their words because they do not sound confident.

Another example - a man may look at a woman and think this woman *loves herself,* not in an arrogant vain way but as an affirmation of one who recognises, unquestionably, her high value. If he believes that of her, how do you think he will treat her? He's going to treat her as she sees herself, therefore he's unlikely to disrespect her, he's going to bring the best version of himself to her because this is a person that demonstrates by her actions the love she has of herself.

People will reflect back at you, who you are; they first have the belief and from that, comes their action. So what is it you believe about yourself?

Stop and think 'What are my I Ams?' Your I Am has the power to take you to higher heights or lower depths. Your I Am will either free you or imprison you. Your I Ams *will* open doors.

I am love, I am wealth, I am abundance, I am peace, I am genius, I am the will of God, I am joy, I am outstanding, I am infinite wisdom, I am enough, I am of sound mind – these are truths of what you might want to finally recognise in yourself.

Every morning when I wake up, I affirm what God sees in me in the mirror by smiling and saying, 'Good morning Beautiful! I am enough!' I am my own best friend. What will *you* affirm about yourself today? No-one can say an 'I Am' for you. It's not just a matter of saying it; remember, it's a matter of you 'embodying it'.

In summary, God's 'I AM' nature dwells within all of His conceptions and The I AM is limitless therefore cannot be limited; God is neither rich or poor, weak or strong, bound or free, male or female as these are limitations of the limitless. Therefore God, The I AM is nameless. To feel yourself to be anything is to manifest an 'I Am' of the nameless, I AM through you.

The NDBRW Method, therefore, serves as the reset required to establish that bridge, in the matrix of your thoughts to allow you the mental space, to pause, re-define and express your I AMs in a conscious way as you press forward to actualise your function.

Perfect in His Sight

From the moment my grand-daughter Mia was born (which coincidentally is an anagram of I AM) my heart sang a chorus of 'You are perfect!' No sane mother looks at her child and thinks 'You're so imperfect!' No, you say 'My child is perfect!'

One day Mia returned from nursery and said, 'Sara doesn't like me.' 'Sara doesn't like you?' I repeated questioningly. 'How does that make you feel?' Mia responds hesitantly... 'It makes me feel sad'. 'Why?' I press gently. 'Because, because, because... Sara wants me to do that thing and I don't want to... Sara doesn't like me... it makes me feel bad'.

Mia had interpreted that there must be something wrong with her for Sara to not like her. Herein begins the change of her self-beliefs from perfect to imperfect, having bought into '*I must be bad.*' Does that mean I see her differently? Does God? *The thoughts God has of you remain perfectly unchanged despite us forgetting.*

I'm concerned she will not always have my voice to counteract any negative conditioning. This time I can pick that seed out of her glass, but what of others? I want her to understand the most important relationship she will ever have is the identity she has in God and to have surety in this.

 I do not want Mia to walk in the energy of '*I am imperfect*' – and yet for this, the world will 'celebrate' her.

The world will celebrate her *modesty* (the quality of being relatively moderate, limited, or small in amount, rate, or level) in downplaying who she really is.

Reader, can you recall a time where you felt so great or so proud of yourself, perhaps for an accomplishment and yet you felt berated for owning it?

We live in a world that bombards us with reinforcements of our supposed imperfection; we tell ourselves we are imperfect because we do not match up with other's expectation. However, what about living up to the expectation of God and recognising the 'I AMs he has written about you?

We were designed and created with free will to choose how we show up but if we choose that which is not in alignment with the will of God, then we create a world of calamity, hurting both ourselves and others. Hurt people, hurt people. So, as God does with all His children, I seek to correct the perception Mia has of herself... and also with you... through the filter of the NDBRW Method.

You see, I know that God does not create copies. God creates originals. **You were created perfectly in the mind of God...and you can't add to that which is already perfect.** The thing is, if you believe yourself to be imperfect then imperfection will breed imperfection, as like produces like.

Therefore, if you believe that you are not enough, then you will believe you need to continuously add to yourself to make yourself complete. Adverts plug into that belief, don't they? They try their best to convince you that if you wear the latest lipstick or trainers, your life will be complete. How absurd!

Church often subscribes to this ideology and capitalise on your 'imperfection'. What about preaching the word **you are already perfect...** and walk in the energy of that? So whatever needs to fall away from you, falls away. In line with the law of I AM, allow the state of cognitive dissonance to do its work. Choose to buy into how God sees you. That is the true reality.

You are perfect, God perfectly packaged you for your purpose and it's with this aim you will walk in truth, knowing you already possess the keys to unlock your destiny.

I know this may feel uncomfortable, but say/feel it out loud 'I am perfect!' and with repetition, have confidence that anything that is not of 'perfection', in time, will fall away from you and align you with that recognition. In Christ, we are all works in this undoing process.

Imagine a world where everyone accepted how God sees them? Not in arrogance but in the truth of their perfection with a deep appreciation of the gifts they can share, rather than just take, of the mentality, that the world doesn't owe them anything.

The sun doesn't ask of the moon: Am I perfect? It just is, and it shares its function with nothing asked in return. The sea doesn't ask 'Am I too emotional with my waves?' It just is. So, it is for us, to accept who we are without question; and drop the beliefs that hide us from our authentic self.

It's a new dawn, only for a finite amount of time and before your time runs out, be bold and step away from any form of false illusion of who you are. Start the process by embracing the NDBRW Method and allow the true you to surface.

In the Bible, when people saw a barren woman in Sarah, God saw the mother of all nations. When people saw a poor young shepherd in David, God saw a mighty King of Israel. When people saw a poor prisoner in Joseph, God saw a powerful Minister of Egypt.

What do you think God sees in you? Trust that it is far beyond that of any human's validation or expectation! God sees you as perfect for the plan He has purposed in you. He sees the truth in you.

WISDOM KEY

What 'I Am's' will you recognise today?

The Source of Personal Power

10. You are Connected

There is no frame...

As I sit in my living room, I draw inspiration for my writing, from a shattered pane of glass, housed within one of the double doors to my back garden. It has been struck hard by a pebble, propelled by the local gardener's lawnmower as he cut the grass.

The glass remains intact, the fragments held together, gleaming brightly as the sun bounces against it, forming a brilliant, beautiful mosaic! We are like fragments of that glass, fragments off God; in essence, perfect to reflect His glory, made in His image.

As I gaze at it, Spirit uses it as a tool to teach me. Each glass fragment, symbolic of the human body, is supported by a myriad of surrounding fragments – each fragment appearing distinct from the other, separate, yet all held tightly together, connected, within its solid frame.

Spirit whispers to me *'when you are in the picture, you cannot see the frame ...'*

God is limitless. He is not limited by time, space or matter.

We live in a world of duality, and through comparison, our perspective based on our perception, through our five senses, allows us to know darkness because we know light. You know silence because you know sound. You know left because you know right. You know up because you know down.

A fish as it dwells, below the deep sea, cannot comprehend the infiniteness within which it swims, because it is part of it. However, I can observe a fish is in the water because I am outside of it. We, therefore, perceive a disconnection through the limitation of our senses... and yet there is a connection.

Why do I now speak of connection? Because in the recognition of our connection, you will recognise your inter-dependent nature and that you must share and support others with all that has been given you - namely your gifts, talents and skills.

Don't think that you are separate...

You are not your body and you are not your mind. You have a body and you have a mind. You are a limitless spirit housed in a body, and if you perceive your body as 'who you are' then you have limited yourself to a cell of your own making.

God's children who have vision are not imprisoned in a body, they see their *limitlessness* through Spirit. They see their energetic interconnectivity like the glass fragments within the frame.

In our understanding of our connectivity, it's easy for us to appreciate that if something is off balance in our body, that the whole body is affected. For example, if you stub your big toe then your whole body is destabilised as our body parts are inter-dependent.

Imagine you go to the doctor with a set of symptoms; it would, therefore, be nonsensical of the doctor to treat the cause and the symptoms as two different things. They are only perceived as separate because the body presents itself as a 'divider'. Without the body, the cause and effect are one and the same. There is no difference.

So why then is it hard for us to understand that outside of the body, the same principle applies cause and effect? We are connected, we are one. What I do, affects you and what you do affects me - for we are one. So as **God looks at us in spirit**, right and wrong are viewed as one - there is no difference.

It is in recognition of this, this oneness, this connectivity; this inter-dependency that you experience a life of heightened empathy. The filter of the NDBRW Method that causes you to see no difference will, therefore, cause you to cultivate and foster a more compassionate attitude towards others, as you see them and yourself as one.

WISDOM KEY
You are interconnected. You are One.

11. God's All-Inclusive Love

Our God is One - He is an inclusive God. He is the Alpha and the Omega - He is the beginning and the end. 'Our Father' the beginning of the Lord's Prayer, tells us of his inclusive nature. No one is exempt.

He includes the rich and the poor, the sad and the happy, the lost and the found, the just and the unjust, the sick and the well, the dead and the living, the black and the white, the rights and the wrongs, the light and the dark...

Do stars not require darkness to shine? All are of equal value to His purpose, which ultimately is the unity of our recognition in Him as Our Father. Anything of equal value to God is the same in God's eyes – there is no difference.

'That ye may be the children of your Father who is in Heaven. For He maketh His sun to rise on the evil and on the good, and sendeth rain on the just and on the unjust.' (Matthew 5:45)

God's inclusive nature exempts no-one and so He does not see you 'singularly' as special, as this would mean to see you as separate.

When God sees us as One, it denies specialness; I believe it better so say that we are unique in His sight; that he loves us uniquely. There is no partiality to His love and we all partake jointly in it. He is so impartial in his love that he gives us perfect justice.

Perfect Justice

His Spirit, ever-present that connects us all, leaves room only for peace; and so fully meets our problems with fairness in its truest sense. The problem is resolved. No one feels hard done by, no one loses – there is no room for an attack of any kind.

The way the world hands out 'so-called justice' however, is where one gains and the other loses, leaving room for the perpetuation of problems, discord and disharmony. In accordance with God's 'all-inclusive' love, no one deserves to lose. As humans, we judge on *effects* but He judges perfectly as he sees *cause*. Hurt people hurt people.

My perception is that our court system is not about justice; as is often the case, it's about revenge. Its concern is political and from my point of view, there's nothing fair about politics... because there's always room for attack.

So we clearly need healing, and healing and restoration are for us all, not kept for some and withheld from those deemed less worthy. NO, all God's children are entitled to restoration and their birth-right.

Perfect justice, *in the view that we are one*, dictates that you reap what you sow; what you give, you receive. In other words, when you give to another, you give to yourself and when you deprive another, you deprive yourself; when you're unjust to another, you are unjust to yourself. Reader, have you experienced that we are connected?

The world we see sacrifices 'oneness' in preference to disunity. If I see you as a separate body from myself, how will I treat you? Will I truly be able to honour the law 'love your neighbour as you love yourself', the second greatest commandment?

Reader, *don't think the judgements that you impose on what you see can limit God in any way.* His laws still stand.

When we live our lives in a Godly way any problems that we have in our relationships we can take to His Spirit and have it resolved in a wholesome way; whereby neither party feels hard done by, that they have lost or gained; and the problem will never raise its head again. The Spirit will look at the wrong or right with equal value and deal with it as one and bring about an outcome that reflects true justice and peace.

To demonstrate this, let's look at a real-life example.

Case in point: One of my Christian friends confided in me that in the early part of her marriage, there was a time that she felt like giving up. She had got married to her husband in her early 20s, they were both university students and she described herself as very headstrong and not easily bossed around!

She explained that at a time of writing a dissertation, her husband, despite her mentioning several times, seemed oblivious of her need for silence. He would have friends around impromptu and being students, they could be quite noisy in their behaviour.

One day, whilst quietly writing and without warning, her husband came home with friends; the noise began and already feeling the pressure of a deadline, she felt a surge of anger well up, ready to spill over... when suddenly she felt prompted by Spirit to hold her tongue!

My friend then got up, served the guests amicably and returned to her desk. A moment later her husband looked across at her, ushered the guests out and approached her, apologising for his insensitivity; all without her saying a word.

Fifteen years later, they are still married and she says 95% of the time; when she remembers, she uses the approach of handing over her problems – her narrow perspective to Spirit to resolve conflict and maintain peace in her marriage.

What you have to know is that God's Spirit lives in His believers and you can only truly experience what you believe, and so Spirit of the name above all names that sees and is the mightiest of all can resolve problems perfectly from His position of ubiquity.

Therefore, trust that when you take conflict and problems to Spirit, Spirit will bridge the gap and prompt you to resolve the situation in a way that brings peace to all parties involved.

So how then do we deal with confrontation in a practical manner? Well, it must first start with *effective* communication with God right at its centre.

Compartmentalising or burying an issue doesn't mean the energy of it goes away; it just causes delay; whilst allowing the problem to take root and grow. That's why it's important to deal with issues head-on and communicate your boundaries before roots of conflict take hold.

Communication with Spirit at the centre is core to every strong authentic connection. When you are made to feel 'wrong' by a person it stops you from trusting them to 'hear' or to respect you. Conflict lives in the energy of I'm right and you're wrong and is THE MOST divisive energy between two or more people.

It causes separation and needs to be addressed before a speed bump becomes a hill and a hill becomes a mountain that is insurmountable. Countless breakdowns and divorces in relationships could have been avoided if dealt with the Spirit's way!

God's Spirit is love and so we must bring His Spirit into our relationships. So let's now look at the 'how to' of resolving conflict and how to effectively resolve negative issues, with Spirit at the centre, which would otherwise cause disconnection.

Moreover if thy brother shall trespass against thee, go and tell him his fault between thee and him alone: if he shall hear thee, thou hast gained thy brother. Matthew 18:15

How to Resolve Relationship Conflict

1. Setting the stage:

Express to the person your wish to have a conversation to enable the both of you to establish a greater connection and have both your needs met - you can say "I want for us to have an opportunity to get back on track, clear the air" or if you're in a romantic relationship you can say "it would make me feel supported if I could just de-charge with you. I'd feel great if you could do that *for me*".

When you can lay aside your ego you make room for Spirit...

2. State your intention:

First open the conversation with what you genuinely, love, admire or respect about the person; for example, I love that you work hard and are committed to saving lives or I respect you for ..." fill in the gap with what you truly *appreciate* about the person.

3. State the facts:

Ensure there is no emotional charge around what you state here, be emotionally centred. State simply the facts. For example, we agreed to meet at 8 pm. You did not turn up for the meeting and I did not receive a call to say you could not make it.

Keep it strictly factual, for if you do not, your conversation will go off at a tangent you did not intend. Don't bring up the past that you cannot change.

4. State your feelings:

When you did that, this is how I felt. I felt frustrated. I felt that my time was unappreciated, I could have organised my morning differently, I'm now feeling overwhelmed.

A person cannot argue with how you feel. How you feel is how you feel, it's your truth and in the expressing of it, you will feel liberated.

Give the person the chance to express their side... They may say words to the effect of... 'This is what happened... I apologise and appreciate where you're coming from..."

5. Make a new agreement

In this case, it could simply be "In the future, I will give you notice if I cannot make it, so you can make appropriate arrangements..." In future, if the agreement is broken, you simply refer back to 'the agreement' which is an entity in itself.

This process can feel *sticky*; however, despite the discomfort, it is necessary to build a bridge and not a wall to enable harmony in relationships, whether it is romantic, platonic or business.

No person is infallible, we have our imperfections and we must give each other the benefit of the doubt, as our perspective may not be as it seems. Additionally, you cannot receive fully from Spirit if you have enmity in your heart. You must clear your cupboard of 'spoils' to receive.

Therefore if you are presenting your offering at the altar, and there remember that your brother has something against you, leave your offering there before the altar and go; first be reconciled to your brother, and then come and present your offering. Matthew 5:23

This kind of conversation saves relationships as it promotes healing and maintains connection and God is all about connection. When you share your perspective it opens the door to be understood; both parties get to express their truth, and the truth will set you free.

God wants us to access and trust Him fully to solve problems, because whatever they may be, to not reach for His spiritual solution is to leave the problem unresolved, devoid of true justice and more room for attack.

The NDBRW Method will cause you to suspend judgement and place you both on a bridge on which you can both share your perspectives and in so doing forgive, reconcile and create unity moving forwards.

God's wisdom to solve is based on His knowing. God knows. God doesn't waiver as we do in making decisions because he knows. And so He guides us, because a confused mind blocks knowledge, therefore true justice. To this aim let's now look to the Scriptures, to another case that illustrates powerfully God's ability to problem solve with wisdom and impartiality.

The Slice of Solomon's Sword

You may be aware of Solomon's famous judgment, 'The splitting of the baby'. We read the account of two women - two perspectives - one claiming the child to be hers, the other not. One was right and the other wrong; both squabbling and in conflict.

Solomon, with the wisdom of God, ordered the soldier to slice the baby in two, so that they could have half each; and as the sword descended, the 'real' mother leapt forward and rather than have her child harmed, offered the baby to the liar.

When God showed up *through* Solomon, Truth showed up! The result... you are the baby's mother. Pick up your baby and walk! Perfect wisdom. Perfect justice, no further perpetuation of the problem - no matter how complex the case. (1 Kings 3:16-18)

God does not look at us on a superficial level; he looks at us deeply and in our entirety. The past, the present and the future;

nothing is hidden. He looks at the truth in us... what he has written in us.

I believe if the circumstances were different, He would have provided another solution. For example, if the birth mother had evil intentions and the other woman had good intentions, God would have seen this.

God looks at your heart and your intent. I believe it wasn't merely because she was the biological mother; it was because her thoughts for the child were in alignment with what He had written for that child. God wants for us, that which He has predestined for us.

Like Solomon, we must allow Gods word to slice through us like a sword. I believe The NDBRW Method is akin to Solomon's word serving as *Solomon's sword* because it can slice through untruths in all areas of life. No matter how you wield the sword, it will always achieve its outcome, because, ultimately the truth will prevail.

WISDOM KEY

God's impartiality gives rise to perfect judgement

12. God is Your Source

God never fails to provide for us, we fail ourselves... When we take on the perceived failures of our own it is important to note that at the point of failure, we now know how to more intelligently begin again. So is it a failure or a win? Unfortunately for the unenlightened, failure is looked upon as doing wrong or viewed as a misfortune, but is it really?

I mentioned that the filter of the NDBRW Method provided me with a level playing field as it dissolved perspectives that limited my potential and curbed me from buying into other people's perspectives that didn't serve me.

There is a Chinese Taoist story that I came across, that will provide you with insight on the importance of opening up the parachute of the mind, and suspending judgement on what we could otherwise perceive as failures or misfortunes.

There was an old farmer who had worked his crops for many years.

One day his horse ran away. Upon hearing the news, his neighbours came to visit. "Such bad luck," they cried shaking their head.

Chewing on a stick of straw the farmer replied. "Hmmm...perhaps."

The next morning the horse returned, bringing with it three other wild horses. "How wonderful, what great luck!" the neighbours exclaimed.

Still chewing on his straw the farmer replied. "Hmmm...perhaps."

The following day, his son tried to tame one of the wild horses, was thrown and broke his leg. The neighbours once again expressed their sympathy for his "misfortune."

The farmer replied, "Hmmm...perhaps."

The day after, military officials came to the village to draft young men into the army but they spared his son because of his broken leg. "What great luck," cried the neighbours!

"Hmmm..." was the farmer's response... "perhaps..."

What's the moral of the story? That maybe we should stop clinging to what we think we know and employ an attitude of non-attachment to judgement. We can't see the whole picture so we can never judge a situation as right or wrong, just 'maybe' or 'perhaps'.

In the story, the perspective of the neighbours was meaningless i.e. it was neither good or bad, wrong or right - because it was based on an incomplete picture. So why get upset or worry? Would you not rather be open to the truth, which means remaining in a state of peace and opening yourself up to a 'maybe' or a 'perhaps'?

God wants us to employ the word 'perhaps' because it opens us up to a myriad of possibilities which expands us all. The moment you say 'maybe' or 'perhaps' you surrender your circumstances to whatever lies outside your understanding - to possibilities that lie outside your paradigm.

When you say 'maybe' or 'perhaps', what you're actually doing is denying the planting of a seed of distrust, denying the impression of another's perception on you. You're not allowing it to take root and suppress potential.

This approach causes us to open up to receiving from God. Whereas judging closes us off to our potential, it makes us *see* only that which we have judged to be right or wrong – therefore limiting us.

God doesn't want us to miss what He's stored up for us. He wants our eyes upwards and open to Him so we can receive our birth-right.

Our growth is expansion and what God creates, grows and flourishes into beauty beyond our wildest imagination!

Living in a world of 'maybe' or 'perhaps' brings us to a place of peace and contentment.

That was, is and always has been, the intention of God.

"For I know the plans I have for you," declares the Lord *"plans to prosper you and not to harm you, plans to give you hope and a future."* (Jeremiah 29:11)

You are Re-Source!

Use your uniqueness as a re-source to another

In the 'Reasoning Exercise, one of the benefits that stood out in the 'dissolving' of the old me, was the ability to appreciate my uniqueness and to understand that no-one can rival me when it comes to being me. No one can stand in my shoes or do things the way I do. They may teach the same subject but will never deliver it the way I do. Why? because I am unique.

I appreciate my gifts are from God and I re-source his gifts to others. *I am His re-source.*

Would I have been able to stand firm in my uniqueness without the filter of the NDBRW Method? I don't believe so. The Method gave me the foundation to realise what that was.

In the movie The Source, Wayne Dyer tells us to take the attention off our self and shift our thoughts, from 'what can I get?' to 'how may I serve?' In other words, how can I serve my uniqueness as a resource to others? God has shown me that in being an active resource to others I will find myself that much more blessed.

Whoever has will be given more, and they will have an abundance... (Matthew 13:12.)

When you serve another, God's universe will serve you with more of what you have served it; remember we are all connected so, at the moment that you give, you get and this constant flow of giving and receiving never ceases.

It's what makes the world go around. If you don't release what is in your hands, you will not provide space for your hands to receive. You need to *circulate your unique gifts, skills and talents.* For example, when I re-source His 'I AM' i.e. my skill as a speaker; its universal law for me to receive more opportunities to speak and for others to receive.

Authors of books and purveyors of information on the internet are re-sources. The creators of the digital distribution platform of my podcasts are re-sources. If they had not appreciated their unique gifts, would I have been able to use them as my resource? What else are my resources?

Well, if you purchased this book you are my resource, as am I to you... Thank you. My mother is my resource. Thank you. My gym instructors are my resource. Thank you. My friends are my resource. Thank you. The shop keeper is my resource. Even the person I don't like that much (for there is something there for me to learn) is my resource and I say, thank you! For in them He re-sources.

It may be as simple as the 'God bless you' from the mouth of a homeless man, as you re-source those coins into his cup or the warmth of a hot cup of coffee on a crisp winter's morning. Look all about you, **everything is a re-source from a God who is our Source.**

Every re-source you receive, give thanks, so that you may receive more abundantly. Every person your eyes alights on is directly or indirectly your re-source. It helps to see everything as a 're-source' as opposed to 'just a resource'; because then you can truly appreciate as you see God in it and feel the connectivity of his nature!

The analogy of the postman

As an Enhanced Relationship Coach, I often have to make clear to women the difference between Source and Re-source. You see, they desire particular qualities in a man, but then when the man falls short, they begin to resent him as they have made the fatal flaw of mistaking him as Source instead of re-source. Let's look at an analogy.

The postman brings you letters but you notice that he's not brought you a letter you're expecting. You don't attack him for not bringing you the letter you want. You accept the letters he has brought you with gratitude.

You may mention you're expecting a letter but not with the mindset that it's his responsibility to bring you the letter - *maybe* that's someone else's job. He cannot give you what he does not have.

If the postman is then delegated to bring the letter to you at a later date, it's because He has been chosen to bring it to you. You will receive it in perfect time, and not because you have demanded it of him.

Your readiness plays a big part...

You will never catch a ball until you are ready to catch it...Spirit.

It's in your acceptance and appreciation of the postman's delivery - his role as your re-source – not Source - that you now make yourself open to more.

In other words, don't shoot the messenger.

God works through us – The letters represent the qualities that you have asked for and the 'postman' the date; the vessel through which your required qualities will be re-sourced. The moment you attach yourself as seeing the postman as *the source* instead of God's re-source; you have bought into an illusion.

Therefore do not focus on what you have not received from him; i.e the 'lack' in him as you will fail to fully appreciate what you have received and so the enjoyment of that will be significantly reduced.

Better you engage in the positive exchange of the giving and receiving of qualities with one another, with deep appreciation, and in so doing you will expand the paradigm of love in which you both participate.

'In everything give thanks, for this is the will of God in Christ Jesus for you.' (1Thessalonians 5:18)

If you looked at every single person God sent your way as a carrier of your good, the answer to a prayer in their unique way, and you gave appreciation of that, imagine where that would take you.

We must appreciate one another as a re-source of God.

Re-Source in Action

DAY 1

It was a Monday and I'd awoken to the ping of my phone with a horrid headache. I think it was because I'd eaten a coconut macaroon the day before, forgetting the fact I have an aversion to it.

Sunday's service was amazing. The children's performance, the singing, the fun, the festivities after, despite the offending macaroon... couldn't lessen it. However what stood out for me was a talk given by a Roy Francis on the history of the church from the Windrush days.

He talked with such zest! He had us leaning forwards in our seat with feelings of nostalgia, his talk finished far too soon. Fortunately, I was able later to purchase his book - *How to Make Gospel Music Work for You.*

The ping of my phone turned out to be a text message from the building society, stating 'You don't have enough money available for payments requested. Please pay money in before 14:30 to ensure payments can be made and to avoid fees'. I checked my account - £5.33. I can't ever remember my account being that low. I got up and swallowed two aspirin and went back to my bed, with the challenge of solving the low funds in my account whilst curled up in a ball under my duvet.

My respite was short-lived as I was disturbed by elevated voices outside my open window; something in the conversation drew me to the ledge and from there I spied a tall, slim good looking black man, mature in age, with a white short beard against his dark skin...maybe ex-army as he was dressed in navy blue combat style with a badge dangling from a string around his neck.

As I looked through the slat of my blinds I could hear my neighbour asking 'Why are you taking a picture of my car? He said 'I didn't', to which she responded, 'But I saw you and I saw you touch it'... He said firmly, 'I didn't, besides this is the car I'm interested in' pointing at my car, as he took pictures of the licence plate and circled it. At one point, for some length of time, he paused to look into my car...maybe he was looking for something to ID me on.

With my head pounding, 'not again' I said wearily to myself 'historic debt has caught up with me.' I texted my best friend, 'Denise, they've come to get my car'. I continued to send her messages such as 'He's got back into his car now, he's walking away...he's coming back. He's gone!' I was in no mood to confront him. Funds were low. My head hurt. My vibe was low. I'll deal with that battle another day. As he disappeared, I could feel the aspirin kicking in, I quickly got dressed and went to the gym to get the blood rushing through my body. My head was heavy but as I moved the cross trainer to and fro, my headache began to shift.

I left the gym an hour later and wondered where I might park my car and perused the surrounding streets looking for a suitable parking spot. I wasn't ready to face the man again but I eventually decided to park outside my home as it would be too obvious if he came back the following day. I knew he wouldn't show... however, my mind was in turmoil and my sleep followed suit.

DAY 2

I wake up and my head is pounding, two days in a row, not as bad as yesterday but it really hurts and I swallow a couple of aspirin again.

I check my car, all is well. I can feel the fear bubbling up inside of me and as I wash a few dishes before heading out, I think I see the man from yesterday and my heart leaps into my mouth, 'Why didn't you leave earlier!' my brain screams, as a regular delivery driver gets out of the van. I'm a nervous wreck. I detest this feeling. This is so far from the usual composed me.

A few minutes later I jump into my car and head to the bank to deposit the little cash I had at home. As I walk from the building society, I pop into McDonald's on Mare Street in Hackney, the east end of London.

I'm not a fast-food kind of girl but I do like their coffee and as I sit there one of the staff members offers me a tray of wrapped buns. She smiles and says they've made too many that morning and are selling them for a pound each. I tell her, 'Unfortunately I don't have any change'. I finish my coffee and leave.

As I walk towards the Tesco car park where I've left my car, I pass two homeless men under the bridge and I think, 'Wouldn't it be great if they had one of those buns?' I feel compelled to get two and so when I get to my car, I retrieve some coins and walk back to McDonald's. As I pass the men, I notice they are both munching on a sandwich each and I think, 'Maybe they're not as hungry as I thought.'

Anyway, I walk to McDonald's and as I'm making my way in, I'm accosted by a black woman who asks me to buy her some chips. I think to myself, 'I'll get her a bun,' however there is only one bun left and as I leave, I hand her the bag, saying 'there are no chips in there but here's a bun,' to which she thanks me.

As I walk back to the car, I drop the remaining pound into the soiled hands of one of the homeless men, and as he expresses an emphatic, 'Thank you! God bless you, Miss!' I feel blessed... abundant even and as I arrive at my car, I hear the familiar voice I recognise, whisper 'You have nothing to fear!'. I repeat 'I have nothing to fear?' questioningly, then as a statement. 'I have nothing to fear!' I knew it was regarding my anxiety over the car.

As I sat in the car I started listening to a YouTube video; I wasn't quite ready to go home and I paused to listen to the video where the speaker was discussing the different ways to identify the law of attraction, explaining that sometimes you have to lose something to gain something and the universe constantly moves the old out of the way to make way for the new.

The message resonated with me and gave me great comfort, I felt renewed in spirit. 'I have nothing to fear' I affirmed. I suddenly felt calm and imagined that maybe the burnt orange Range Rover Evoque Cabriolet was on its way! The video reminded me to not be attached to anything, however - let Go and let God.

My phone pings again, it's a text from a friend asking how I am? I had texted him earlier to say my head hurt. It would be soothing to see him and he promises to pop by in a couple of hours.

I return home fearless, prepared to accept God's will over my life. My headache is now a very dull ache in the background. I briefly visit my sister who is in recovery from cancer and is undergoing radiotherapy. She's in good spirits today and I return home a few hours later, in time for my friend's visit.

When he asks me why I'm so stressed, I only tell him part of the story. How can I possibly share with him that I have £5.33 left in my account and I'm about to lose my car? I do not want to be viewed as irresponsible. So I tell the story of the coconut and use this as the reason for my two-day-long headache.

That night I fall asleep, in faith, not fear, calm not turmoil. Having reaffirmed that just because I have thoughts of anxiety, doesn't mean I have to believe in it or act on them. I can choose to think differently - I have nothing to fear.

DAY 3

Expectantly and with no surprise, I wake to the sound of the jangling of chains. I already know what and who, it is. As I peek through the window, I can see the man has returned and is fastening the chains of the clamp to my car. But this time when I look, there is no fear. I am calm and accepting of what fate comes to me. I have nothing to fear and am unattached to the outcome.

The man has knocked on my neighbour's door. This time he asks her if I am the owner, nodding his head at my door. She does not respond but calls out to me from her back door, I'm now in the living room and she tells me the man is back. I tell her that I know and not to worry.

As I take my time to get dressed to meet him, with no anxiety at all...he calls out through my letterbox and threatens 'They're going to tow your car away'. I now feel centred. I tell myself I will not allow any circumstance to dictate my mood and that it's a great morning because this is just part of the process of God answering my prayers. I am ready.

I leave my front door and walk towards his car, he is writing something and doesn't see me until he hears my voice. In a low tone, I greet him with a 'Hey, good morning, you've been looking for me?' He looks at me and replies: 'Good morning, are you the owner of that car?" I answer, 'Yes I use it, it's under the company name' and nod at the paperwork in his hand. 'Tell me, how much is outstanding?'

He responds: Do you have any ID?' I raise an eyebrow as if to say 'really, you think I want to be having this conversation?' I remain silent. He then proceeds to tell me the outstanding amount - £710. Even though I've centred myself, I begin to feel kind of emotional and I rein back unshed tears. I say calmly, 'I cannot pay that amount'. Can I pay in instalments? 'No', he replies, but then after a sigh, offers to knock £235 off.

I say calmly 'I cannot even manage that much, to tell you the truth, I was expecting you. I saw you on Monday but I wasn't in the frame of mind to talk to you. I'm prepared to let the car go. It's out of my hands now; I leave in the hands of God'.

We both pause in a brief moment of silence.

Then he says 'I knew you were a Christian'.

With a raised eyebrow I reply 'Really? How do you know that?' He said, 'On Monday, I looked into your car and I saw a book written by Roy Francis. I know Roy Francis. I produce gospel music too'. I laugh and he laughs too as I say, 'What a small world!'

He says: 'I'll tell you what, why don't you go inside? I'll come back to you shortly'.

I go back to the house and make a cup of tea and a short while later, there is a knock on the door. It is the man and he says, 'I'm going to take the clamp off your car'. This time, unchecked tears flow down my cheeks - I know it was God!

He says 'You can pay in instalments and I advise that you do because if any other officer catches you out there, you'll be in the same predicament. However I'm going to walk away, I'll call you in a couple of weeks, see where you're at. Give you some time to get yourself together'.

'But before I go, I want to give you one of my CDs'. It is a Gospel CD and a flyer to one of his gospel events taking place the next month. I thank him as he bids me farewell. His last words to me are 'You are blessed'.

The homeless man under the bridge said 'God bless you' and here was this Christian Officer saying, 'You are blessed'.

One mouth extended the blessing, the other mouth delivered the blessing.

It was after I gave the homeless man the little that I had that I received. In my giving, I had received.

I was his re-source; this officer had become my re-source.

Thank you Source.

I was overcome with the emotion of wonder and awe. I texted Denise, who is not a Christian, telling her how God had come through for me. I wanted her to know God is real, that He still shines brightly for us all.

I jumped into my car a few minutes later to head to the gym, I felt amazing! I popped the CD he had blessed me with in the deck. It blew me away; it was the most beautiful music I'd ever heard. The first track was called 'You are so beautiful.' I played track two, four times in a row after parking outside the gym. It was so good! I felt so blessed!

After leaving the gym I approached Asda supermarket. In a trolley outside the store, someone had left their recently bought toothpaste behind. I took it in to the store, handed it to customer services and said, 'Just in case the person comes back' and then felt a sudden urge to buy a lucky dip lottery ticket.

That night I slept amazingly well.

DAY 4

I feel amazing. I've had a good night's sleep. I check my lottery ticket - I've won the lottery! Well, it's two numbers, entitling me to a free lottery ticket. It's not the jackpot but it's something. I hang onto the 'something'. I am a winner! That is the vibe that I choose to carry with me today.

Reader, this may seem like a small thing, but when you count your something as nothing, even that will be taken away from you. I choose to count it as something.

'Whoever has will be given more, and they will have abundance. Whoever does not have, even what they have will be taken from them' (Matthew 13:12)

Always believe that you have and it's in the gratitude of the little that you have, that more will be given to you.

WISDOM KEY

Adopt a 'maybe' mentality and receive the best from God

Make Your Potential Visible

13. Competence

How competent are you?

You were never designed to be competent at everything, that is God's job. It's conceited to think that as a human being you can be fully competent independent of God. However, what you could be highly competent at is being the unique you.

People, blind to this truth walk around like zombies, the living dead, and do not know or realise how truly brilliant they are; diamonds in the rough, they compare themselves to others, thinking they are living an authentic life. If they walk with the filter of The NDBRW Method, it will start to awake them to the real life, as God intended it.

For what is the 'perceived' real? How do you define real? If you're talking about what you can feel, smell and taste and see with your senses, real is simply the interpretation of electromagnetic particles all around us. We're energetic (physical) beings with a spirit that's capable of so much more.

However, when you see yourselves as incomplete and broken, how do you treat others with this belief? You see others also as broken, something to be fixed. What truths can spring from the broken? And so, the cycle continues - the perceived broken trying to fix the broken.

With this energy of brokenness and incompleteness, it was inevitable that evil entered this world because we are not walking in the way God intended. God will restore your sight if you allow him. He is a God of vision thus great compassion.

In society, we observe people who we can see are physically whole, all limbs are intact and yet, they have this insane idea they are physically incomplete and so they walk in that e-motion (energy in motion) seeking a 'fix,' an operation to satisfy body dysmorphia, an illusion – an insanity - an untruth. God doesn't see what doesn't exist, he sees you the way he created you.

We have an epidemic where people do not accept what basic biology dictates. They embrace feelings that tell them otherwise and if this is not enough, they want us to join into the insanity and view them in the way they see themselves. If they say they are a rabbit, ought we to address them this way? When will the absurdity end?

Just yesterday I read a case of a young man wanting to sue a clinic for not asking him the appropriate questions before he made a sex change and now regrets it! There is NDBRW in a world of insanity, in a world of illusion all insanity is of equal value, there is no difference.

God is a healer and of miracles. I advise you to take any feelings, that are in contradiction to the will of God, to His Spirit in conversation and trust He will resolve it for you. I will give you a guideline on how to do that in the last chapter of this book.

God Gave us Meaning

We need to stop clinging to what we think we know. That voice within us which I will refer to as 'The Insidious' wants you to think there is a difference between right and wrong because it wants you to miss the truth!

Reader, please know:

1. The voice of The Insidious doesn't want you to see the truth.
2. The Insidious wants you to squabble in this illusionary world over the difference between right and wrong because it wants you focused on **conflict** on **divisiveness** and for you to miss peace.
3. It wants you to make judgements of what's right and what's wrong and judgements determine what you see.
4. It wants you to **miss the truth of who you truly are** and keep up the mindset of who you think you are.

The same insidious voice said to me: 'Is it really so that there is no difference between right and wrong?' Where have we heard that tone before?

What did the serpent say in the story of Adam and Eve... "is it really so that if you eat of the tree of life and death you will know good and evil?"

'For God knows that when you eat from it your eyes will be opened, and you will be like God, knowing good and evil.' (Genesis 3:4)

Liar!

This tells us that from Eve's perspective that she did not know of any difference. She held the view - God's view that *there is **no** difference between right and wrong* in the reality He created; until the Serpent suggested otherwise. The devil is a liar.

The concept of right and wrong did not exist, only oneness until the serpent's intervention.

Spirit says:
"the moment you closed your eyes to me, you were rendered incompetent to see the true picture".

The NDBRW Method is here to reset you. When you walk in the lie that there is a difference between right and wrong you walk in an untruth, on a road that leads to death, death to the fullness of the abundance of your being - death to your birth-right.

The Insidious wants us to attach false meanings. Of itself, nothing has any meaning except that which you give it; if you call a thing wrong, it is wrong and if you call it right, it is right...to you... but it doesn't necessarily make it the **truth.**

God created us and gave us meaning. God gave us purpose, and without purpose, we do not exist. It is purpose that created us, purpose that connects us, purpose that pulls us, guides us and defines us. It is *written...* God wrote his purpose on us when He designed and created us.

Consider this, when the car was first created it was given meaning, a purpose by its creator. The car did not give itself meaning, *for it is written...* the creator of the car wrote its meaning.

When we are confused over the wrongness and the rightness of our purpose, we attempt to write our meaning on ourselves which leads to our downfall.

Release the Images

The aim of this book is to release perceptions that limit us and free our minds of the negative images that grip us. Ultimately, we are the 'image-makers' and the world that we see are the effect of the images that we hold in our mind. In essence, we bend reality to 'shape' that which we hold in our mind. We are the cause. When you can let go of false perceptions, it is then you will be able to see what is real.

Have you ever gone to a place to get something you know is there but you cannot find it? One day I went to my cupboard to get the salt and I couldn't see it. I closed the cupboard door, walked away because I was getting frustrated and turned my attention to other stuff before returning to the cupboard, not with the intention to find the salt but there it was, right there in front of me. It had been there the whole time!

The salt I had bought a few days prior was in a new unfamiliar packaging, I'd picked up a different brand to my usual one so I didn't recognise it. You see, what we do is we look outwardly for the image that is a match to the one we hold in our mind. If it is a mismatch we do not see it. Coincidentally... how often do we do that when seeking our ideal partner? He or she is right there but we miss out because of the packaging.

Now, what actually happened when I walked away and I started doing different things? My mind unattached itself from the image I held of the salt and in doing so, I was now *open* to seeing the salt, to seeing the truth.

When you're attached to the images you see in your mind, you cannot see what is right in front of you. The real world is right in front of you. If you let go and become unattached from how you see the world you would receive a life of abundance.

The time is always *now* to release the thoughts that have you shackled to looking at your place in the world in a limiting way. You need to un-attach yourself from the thoughts, the judgements that limit and prevent you from fully actualising you. It is *time to make your potential visible* and allow it to open doors that no one can shut because God has designed you a particular way.

'I know your works. Behold, I have set before you an open door, which no one is able to shut. I know that you have but little power, and yet you have kept my word and have not denied my name.' (Revelation 3:8)

Ultimately, you see the world you have made but you do not see yourself as the image-maker - you have to realise you are the image-maker. You cannot escape from the world but you can escape from the cause. You are the cause and you have the power to change it.

Remain in God's Hands

There's a scene in the film The Matrix where the Oracle tells Neo that he is not The One. The spin-off from that statement will make him into The One. This means:

1. Neo began self-searching and questioning 'Is he *The One* or is he not?'

2. He sees himself finally as indeed connected to all things – he is not separate.
3. He becomes The One, One that sees Truth.

This is a film with much spiritual depth and wisdom.

I wrote this book because I believe that through my experience you will be set free on so many levels, realise your oneness and be released from beliefs that have held you back from your true function.

It is paramount that you recognise God's hand at work in your life. God planted this message in me for a reason – to bring this message to you. God has re-sourced His message through me. I Am His messenger.

God will direct you to hear this message; and at the appointed time, if you give Him your ear, He will mould and conform you to fulfil your function because you are an arrow of his making, perfectly poised in His hands, ready to make your mark.

For this, He requires your pliability and flexibility in His hands, through your 'maybes' and that includes being comfortable with silence to the rights and wrongs of this world and open to hearing the truth of the Spirit as He restores your mind.

Reader, it's my calling that I do my part in directing you to the path of your abundance. That is your birth-right, instead of the illusionary path of descending madness. Stop resisting Him and look at what leaning on your own understanding has brought you so far and make a decision to follow the direction of the voice of Spirit that resides in every one of us; recognising that the peace of God is with you always.

When you allow God to match you to your purpose and use all your, gifts, talents and skills that are a match for it, your 'enoughness' will open doors that no one can slam shut and you will find it the most rewarding thing ever. Don't be afraid to be you. Embrace NDBRW and walk with energy in the faith of where it will take you.

As I creep closer to the final chapters of this book, the words 'it is enough' springs to mind. It may have its flaws but it is enough. You have your flaws but you are enough. To say that you are enough means it is not a *mistake* that you are who you are, in this space, place and time; you are not here by accident. You are here on purpose and perfectly packaged for it.

The time has come for you to make a choice dear reader. Will you choose to live in God's vision and make a difference?

Your voice matters.

WISDOM KEY

Becoming competent means releasing 'incompetency'

Personal Potential in Action

14. Your Voice Matters

The NDBRW Method is a conduit to you finding your voice

Throughout this book, I've often alluded to a troubled past. Why did I have low self-esteem? What made me feel my voice wasn't valid? Why did I not express my feelings? What led me to write this book?

Well, I want to answer those questions with the intention that it brings hope to those who are where I was. I want you to know that light can be brought to a very dark place.

Looking back on my childhood I would describe my upbringing as somewhat traumatic - several incidents caused me to suppress my voice as I felt my truth didn't matter. My experience of 'sharing my feelings' was of abuse, hurt and pain.

I recall one incident when I was about 10 years of age and at home with my family.

We regularly gathered together to watch television but on one occasion, the TV set had been moved upstairs and placed in a corner to punish us for some misdemeanour. I didn't want to miss my favourite programme so I snuck quietly upstairs, removed its sheet covering and drew the telly forwards to the front of the landing, propping myself on the steps to watch.

One by one, all of my nine siblings joined me and we sat huddled together on the stairway; all of us engrossed in our favourite weekly show. Now for a house that is usually bustling with noise and children running around, the silence alerted my parents that something was 'up' and it wasn't long until we heard our father's heavy footsteps making their way ominously up the stairs.

We had been watching the TV without his permission and what followed next will forever remain etched in my mind. It was horrendous and traumatic for me to witness and be a part of.

As he pounced upon us, my dad drew his belt from his waist and began to beat every one of us. Among the cries and the welts that appeared on our skin, he kept barking, 'Who moved the TV'?' None of us confessed and I certainly wasn't about to as I didn't want to suffer any more pain!

He violently persisted, as he was determined to get to the bottom of it, and as we all cowered in the corner and cried from the blows of the belt as it descended on our heated skin; my dad decided to single out two of my younger brothers.

With deftness and skill, he began to lash them with the belt over and over, as if he was trying to break a runaway slave...with the constant yell of 'Who moved the TV?' ringing in my ears.

Just as I noticed he was getting tired... my brother spent and broken and with nowhere to run whispered, 'It was me... I moved the TV.' My dad demanded, 'Say it again'. My brother dutifully repeated, 'I moved the TV', it was like a scene out of the movie 'Roots - My name is Toby!'

My dad, now victorious, dropped the belt and cried out triumphantly, 'Yes! I knew it! I knew it was you!' At this point, my other little brother stood up with his chest puffed out and despite his obvious pain, stood steadfast and said, 'I did not move the TV' and my dad, in turn, accused him of helping my other brother! My brother was determined to speak his truth!

As a child, I felt guilty knowing I was the culprit and had contributed to my brothers' pain...but I was too scared to speak the truth. I had witnessed the effect of speaking your truth and it so frightened me, I suppressed my voice.

There were many more incidents, each reinforcing my view that my voice was worthless. Looking back, I believe my late Father had mental sickness, could anyone be so wicked? I was taught to walk in the lie that my voice didn't matter, my cry didn't matter, my pain didn't matter and this belief affected all my relationships.

It was no surprise then, that in my early 20s, I attracted a man who both physically and psychologically abused me. He spoke abusive words, too demeaning to share and although I knew it to be wrong, I tolerated it.

At the time, I didn't realise I had been taught low self-esteem through the behaviour of my parents. At 23 I began counselling after receiving a leaflet delivered through my door. The message resonated deeply, as it offered services to young adults who had been abused. I knew I had to make the call.

Through my counselling, I came to several understandings. First, because I was taught not to express my feelings as a child, I was unable to give voice to my truth - my voice remained trapped, having proved worthless as a child; this simply carried through into my adulthood and subsequently my relationships.

Secondly, I tolerated abuse because it was 'familiar' to me and so I attracted an 'emotionally unavailable' man because my father was of this disposition and lastly... my biggest insight was that...

Even though lost it hadn't lost its value - **my voice** *hadn't lost its value!*

Much like in *Luke 15:8-10* where a woman is described as sweeping her house clean in search for a coin that, even though lost, hadn't lost its value, it had just lost its usefulness.

I wanted to be 'useful' and learnt that to do so I would have to value my voice. I learnt my opinion was just as valid as the next person's and as I began with baby steps to express my voice, my self-worth slowly crept up. Eventually, the abused woman, who attracted that abusive man, fell away and so too did the relationship.

I took charge and embraced my personal and spiritual development. I learnt how my energy and my psychological blueprint (my vibe) played a role in attracting men who were a reflection of me.

I was to later learn about the Law of Attraction which states 'that which is like unto itself is drawn'. I prefer to more accurately quote from Matthew 13:12 *'If you have, then more will be given unto you.'* In other words, if I build myself up more in His identity then more of that 'build-up' will be given to me.

I was determined to have better. I was hungry for answers - I was seeking a message from the mess. It was from this my Spirit gave me the words...'To Know the Difference between Right and Wrong, knowing the path of restoration it would set me on. I needed spiritual healing and no man-made clinic could have restored me.

> [8] *'For my thoughts are not your thoughts,*
> *neither are your ways my ways,'*
> *declares the LORD.*
> [9] *'As the heavens are higher than the earth,*
> *so are my ways higher than your ways*
> *and my thoughts than your thoughts'* (Isaiah 55:8-9)

What healing do you need?

Now, I don't know your story, but what I do know is that maybe you've created a tower of your own making, maybe you've been through some kind of trauma or abuse and I guess, maybe you're not walking in the best version of yourself and getting the best out of your relationships, of a romantic nature or otherwise. To some extent, maybe you've lost your voice but I'm here to tell you, your voice matters.

I know my perspective at the time created a tower around me to protect me. I had become a Rapunzel of my own making. However, as I got wiser, I saw my perspective had me shackled and stopped me from healthily interacting with others. I desperately longed to escape its prison.

You see, the inner shame, feeling of unworthiness and not feeling 'good enough' permeated everything around me.

At the time, I felt if people could truly 'see me', they would find me unworthy of their company.

The brave 10-year-old me created her perspectives, her narratives, her beliefs to protect me; I am so grateful for her strength and her tenacity. However, I had to let her story go and replace it with one that better served me in realising my unique purpose!

This purpose includes connecting with others - and to connect with others, I had to first have the courage to fully connect with myself and to do this I needed to knock down the walls of my Rapunzel.

I began to see His light and pull up the weeds of beliefs that were stifling my potential; I began to see myself as God sees me. In changing my story, to 'I am worthy', the universe bent my reality to my 'I am'. I was planting new seeds of 'I am' and reaping the benefits. I didn't believe I was enough to be loved, just as I am. However, I now walk in confidence that God loves me, just as I am, just as he created me.

The intervention of The NDBRW method released me from my shackles and made me realise that I couldn't expect others to see me if I couldn't even see myself. It shone a spotlight on me, making me visible to both myself and others. When your authenticity shows up, people recognise your light and it goes before you.

Embracing my voice hasn't been easy but it's been worthwhile. Embrace your voice; it's been waiting for you. Have the courage to be vulnerable, uplift it from the dark and love your voice with all your 'heart'. You will find the compassion you have with yourself leads to your compassion for others; and when you lead with authenticity, you will receive that from others. The Spirit will use your healing and extend it to others.

So what is the alternative? if you do not forgive yourself of your negative self-judgements, you will be forever kept on a perpetual circle of attracting like judgements from yourself and others, to validate the lowliness you feel about yourself.

Forgiveness is the crux of dissipating all pain. Forgiveness of my father was not condoning or saying what he did was OK, it was about breaking the chains to my past and freeing me to purposefully move forwards into my birth-right of abundance. It is in the willingness to let go of the ball and chain that you allow the authentic you to shine through. Your courage, vulnerability and forgiveness are the springboards for your peace, freedom and voice!

I want for you, as I did for myself, to approach life feeling worthy. I want you to express your unique voice and approach life with boldness and a feeling of deserving; with a sense of worthiness that spills into every area of your life.

I believe that every voice matters. It is my 'why' I wrote this book. I believe that when you can release and make an impact with your unique voice, it is then that you will truly see and believe that your voice matters.

Don't bury your weapon, your voice is your weapon; use it to fight the good fight.

"Never let anyone define you. You are the only person who defines you. No one can speak for you. Only you speak for you. You are your only voice." Actor: Terry Crews

Your Feelings are a Voice

Recognising your authentic voice!

We have this expression 'speak your mind' and I think, in the main, we see this in the 'masculine'. However, for women, I believe, 'speak your feelings' has been more nurtured within us and therefore society views us as 'emotional creatures'. I believe to speak your feelings, is to speak your heart and to speak your heart is to speak your voice'.

Metaphorically speaking, your feelings are a voice –
a language that speaks directly to God and his universe.

No matter your colour, race, culture or creed we all have feelings and your feelings are your true authentic voice. It is this that God's universe responds to, your energy in motion (emotion) the vibration you project into the universe and from this, you cannot hide.

From the way I was raised, I was literally trained to suppress my feelings - my voice, and as I grew up in that environment and eventually into an adult, I found myself in a constant state of non-alignment, where my verbal voice didn't match my feeling voice.

As an adult, it didn't serve me to not express what I really felt. I was shy and being shy limited and diminished my potential. So I consciously learnt how to give voice to my feelings and believe in its validity. I am still learning.

To effect this change, I've had to treat my feelings almost as a separate entity, and ask my feelings, 'what would you have me say?' and stand up for my feelings. What are your feelings saying right now?

138   VALERIE A. CAMPBELL

Your feelings want to say what's on 'its mind.' Your feelings want to be acknowledged, they want to be voiced. They want to be heard! What is in your heart? Will you be bold and allow your authentic voice to be expressed and take centre stage or be suppressed?

Reader, life is too short; it's important to pay attention to how you feel, as it indicates whether you are on track to what you want, or do not want. If you do not like how you're feeling, ask yourself 'what do I want?' This will give you a feeling of positivity to 'receive' what you want. Your feelings serve as an emotional barometer.

The moment you start to suppress your feelings, you suppress your truth. Start to practise using the words 'I feel' in your conversations and express positively. In situations, ask yourself, how do I feel about this? Analyse and speak your feeling. People can feel when you're speaking your truth and it will permit them to do the same.

Furthermore, people can receive healing when they express their feelings; and when one receives healing, they can offer healing to another. You cannot give what you do not have; so whatever healing you need in another, you must first heal within yourself. The NDBRW Method will facilitate this.

Today I attended the ICAN church in London and whilst I stood there stewarding at reception, one of the Ministers came out and expressed to the videographer, who wanted a quick sound bite of his talk on camera, that he was nervous. He said: 'I have cotton mouth – I feel nervous, I don't know quite what to say to the camera.'

It was endearing and as I watched him, I noticed his ability to be vulnerable and I loved it. It was touching, it was real and it was authentic. It was a silent acknowledgement that internally we are all the same. A silent permission for us to do anyway, and so he did, he overcame and delivered his talk good *enough*.

No Mr Right and No Mr Wrong

In my understanding that God...

- wants us to access Him and not lean on ourselves to resolve our problems;
- that His Spirit will work through us to serve and help each other to resolve problems;
- wants us to use our uniqueness as a resource to others;
- reach and use our authentic voice to permit others to do the same;

I reached again for a place of stillness.

I'd not too long written my first book, *She's Got That Vibe*, under the direction of The Voice, within which I spelt out some home truths for women who date. In my desire to share my concepts with as many women as possible, I knew it was important to stand out in the marketplace.

As I sat quietly on the side of my bed, I asked Spirit, 'What is my unique selling point? How do I make myself stand out from all the other Coaches out there teaching insights into spirituality, break-ups, feminine energy and self-esteem in the field of dating?' An area in which I most needed to learn, thus educate.

As I pondered this, Spirit's voice softly intervened, reminding me that there is no difference between right and wrong. What was the link between this and dating? What was I missing?

The penny suddenly dropped... of course, there is no difference between Mr Right and Mr Wrong! There is just one's perspective. Whilst the media were teaching 'How to get your Mr Right?' I was to speak the truth and say there is no such thing.

You see... despite what you've been told, there is no such thing as Mr Right and there is no such thing as Mr Wrong! Energetically speaking, you always attract your perfect match because you can never attract more than how you feel about yourself. Sadly, many women aren't happy with what they are attracting and do not know how to break this pattern.

This truth forms the basis of my coaching. For, if you deem him Mr Wrong, are you not then Ms Wrong? And if you deem him Mr Right are you not then Ms Right? So you **attract who you are and not what you want.** You attract what you see through your perspective. Your beliefs.

Your perspective determines how you see. You give meaning to what you see. If you call a thing wrong it is wrong, if you call it right it is right. The thing in itself is neutral. It is your interpretation of a person that determines whether they are a match or not to the way you want to feel.

Your interpretation, based on the perception you have of yourself can be changed – therefore your results can too. One woman's interpretation makes her see a man as Mr Right whilst another, Mr Wrong.

One man's food is another man's poison, it's all in how you view this from within your glass, from your filter of beliefs.

When you understand this, you live at the cause of what you're attracting. You say to yourself, 'I'm the one that's attracting that! It's not happening to me. I am not a victim. I am the cause and that is the effect' as you see the cause and effect as one. So if you're the cause and you're not happy with what you're attracting then there's something about your perception that needs to change. No one is responsible for your interpretation, but you.

So Reader, let's look at you.

When you look at yourself, know that you cannot attract more than how you feel about yourself, beyond your perception of self. So how you feel deep down? If you say to yourself, 'I don't feel worthy, I don't feel I am enough - you will never attract more than your paradigm allows - you will only attract the familiar and what you're comfortable with, within your comfort zone.

If you're familiar with abuse, you will attract it until you grow to a place where you are no longer comfortable with that; and this happens when you start treating yourself better, therefore, opening your paradigm to other possibilities. This happens when you give voice to your authentic wants and set boundaries and take direction from Spirit. It is then that you will begin to attract an authentic match to yourself.

This fruit of the NDBRW Method has empowered and freed many women, as they realise to attract their ideal match, that change is required within.

The NDBRW Method gave birth to my unique 'Vibes Formula' – a unique proven programme to help women become the authentic match to the type of man they want to attract. V.I.B.E.S. is an acronym for Vision, Intention, Beliefs, Expectation and Sustain as these are the attributes that require change.

You are the most important person in a relationship and if you're not happy with the opinion you have of yourself, how do you expect someone to be truly happy with you in a relationship? If you're not comfortable with being yourself, how do you expect another to be happy in your company?

It's important that you see yourself as God originally intended and make no apologies for that. Take counsel/coaching and correct the vision you have of yourself and face up to who you are and your authentic desires.

Albert Einstein said *'you cannot solve a problem with the same mind that created it.'* The NDBRW Method will allow you to take off the mask you present to others whilst the V.I.B.E.S formula will take you on a journey to stand strong in your authenticity.

When you fall short of your authenticity, you lose who you intrinsically are and will only ever attract people or circumstances that match the mask you wear. This means who or whatever is ultimately predestined for you, you will not be in alignment to receive.

So ask yourself, 'Who am I? What is it that I truly want? How do I want to feel in a relationship?' Keep pressing forward. Ultimately, you want to feel love for you, so ensure you work on loving yourself, making it visible and you will attract in its likeness.

'Love your neighbour as yourself. There is no commandment greater than these.' (Mark 12:31)

Don't be afraid to voice it, own it, wear it and be it, in the very fibre of your being. Remember you attract who you are. You polarize, then magnetise. Don't be afraid to polarise people. Be bold, brave and assertive. In doing so, you will attract what is for you and repel what is not. That is polarisation.

As part of attaining your vision, take control of the part of your life that you can control and start to rein in your wayward thoughts - focus on what you want more of in your life. Don't embrace feeling small to make other people comfortable about their feelings of inadequacy. Don't dim your light to fit the judgement of another. Don't rob yourself of reaching your highest potential, for this life is but a passing dream.

Choose to shine at your brightest. Choose happiness. When you have freed yourself of the opinions of others, you are free indeed.

WISDOM KEY

Own your feelings and you own your voice

Closing Remarks

15. Summary

I t's almost as if my life's work, so far, has directed me to receive, step into and prove first the truth of the NDBRW Method before presenting it to you. I had to be the difference to bring a new perspective.

So... how do you be the difference? You have to become the difference.

Becoming the Difference

At the time of writing, I asked Spirit 'Why did you make me write this book, **The Difference**, now and not before She's Got That Vibe?

I have mentioned previously that I received the message NDBRW before I penned She's Got That Vibe and I questioned the order of writing as it didn't make sense to me.

Spirit responded *"I made you write this book now as I had to have you as a walking example of the fruits of the NDBRW Method"*

Spirit continued...

"When you found out there was NDBRW it made you stop buying into other people's judgement so easily, it strengthened you to buy

into mine, which gave you a level playing field; because of that you were then able to write 'She's Got That Vibe' (SGTV) because I needed you to have that vibe that NDBRW will give you and believe in the validity of your voice!

You used your non-judgemental voice to calm others and have them open up to you – you became their coach... their counsellor. And as you began to believe more in the usefulness of your voice you embraced becoming an international speaker and personality of your own radio show to become more. Every single week you speak! Had you not embraced the methods of NDBRW would those things have happened? There is order in your destiny...

*I had to make you **a walking example of 'your difference'**- a fruit of the NDBRW Method so that when you go out and speak on the contents of this book a person will look at you in your difference and think 'What do I see?'*

I see Valerie as authentic and bold. I see a woman who is a best-selling author, a Radio Show and TV Personality with millions of streams per month. I see an Inspirational Speaker. I see a transformational and articulate teacher...and why? Because you have found your voice, powerful, through this message I've given to you...and you will become more...now, this message you will extend to others.

*And so in answer to your question, **that's why** I made you write SGTV before this book... in preparation for your function... these are the fruits of my message"*

Sometimes we can't see or even understand the order in which God does things. It makes no sense to us because we're in the picture. However, God is outside the picture and is guiding our movements preparing us for our function to fulfil His purpose, when we allow Him.

I am His function, as are my hopes for you. A digit on His hand. A part of the body of Christ; and if you put your trust in Him He will have you fully-fledged for your function and prepared for your flight... It's your turn to be the difference.

Be the Difference

In reading this book, you have gone through the process of becoming the difference. You are being awakened. By wearing the filter of The NDBRW Method you will have expanded your awareness and shifted your paradigm to a new sphere of joy and freedom.

The first part of applying The NDBRW Method is to receive it in the way I received it. Have you become *still minded* in the reading of this book? One of the questions that may have occurred to you is *'How do I hear Spirit?'* Well, you have to learn to become still on a regular basis. To be still is to have a mind clear of conscious thinking.

Recently I came across a term called 'clairaudience' which refers to a gift or an ability to receive auditory information through psychic and sixth sense hearing. This perfectly describes my ability.

On further research, I discovered it falls under the description of ESP – Extra Sensory Perception. I believe we all have ESP, senses that lie outside of our five 'normal' senses and that one just needs to learn to tap into it.

As mentioned I believe we 'hear' because we first hear spiritually. We see because we first 'saw' spiritually. We speak because we first spoke spiritually.

Our physical representation of such is merely prosthetics.

Begin the process...

Practice meditation and be still, this is not about being in analytical mode; this is about allowing thoughts to flow through you whilst in that state of stillness and not allowing you or any distracting thoughts to get in the way. To get into oneness with the Spirit, you can say: 'I am quiet. I am still. I am ready to hear.'

'Be still and know that I am with you' (Psalm 46:10)

These are my personal steps:

a. I see Spirit as a warm and personal friend; never as a 'title' – 'The Spirit', so invite Spirit in with intention. You may say inwardly 'I am ready to hear you'.

b. I provide the space to have a conversation - I allocate the first hour of my day to do this.

c. Spirit comes first - absolutely no checking of messages on phone. I need my mind pure of any distraction so I'm 100% present. I don't want 'conscious thought' to get in the way.

d. I'm ready to hear from Spirit – in a mode of expectancy i.e. open to receive/hear and engage in conversation.

e. In the stillness and the gentleness of my mind, I let go and allow the words to come and flow through me and converse with me.

f. I most often spark a conversation by reading something inspirational, the Bible, the word of God.

g. I ask questions, sometimes before I go to bed, so it's a follow-through of a conversation.

h. The answer begins to come to me as I hear my Spirit respond, like a soft pressing in my mind like footsteps in the sand.

i. Soon I am in flow and receive bursts of insights, inspiration, direction and sometimes visions which I capture by recording on my phone app or by writing down what I hear..

j. I do this daily.

Learning Points:

1. Through your Spirit, you can 'bend reality' and you are doing so every day with the power of your energy in motion - vibrations are the projected force behind your goals, the energy you use to communicate with God's universe every day 24/7. Yes! Even in your sleep, you shape your reality.

2. I believe we came here to 'experience' and to leave a mark - we were born with in-built with questions that drive us. What are your questions? They will drive you to the unfolding of your purpose. It is the questions that drive us.

3. To enable the answer to your question(s) is to get into a state of 'maybe'. 'Maybe' opens you up to possibilities beyond your perspective, your wildest imagination. Living in a world of 'maybe or perhaps' will bring you to a place of peace, love and contentment.

4. You must be willing to go on the flow of Spirit's direction and not your imagined understanding or the perspective of others.

5. You have to walk in faith and not fear – both are two sides of the same coin and whatever you give your focus to, you

will attract. Choose your perspective wisely; ensure it is in line with the will of God.

6. Get God's word in you. If you noticed, I've cited many scriptures throughout this book because His word is in me and Spirit will bring it to the fore when you most need it. Keep building yourself up in His word.

7. Writing this book has been a process as dictated by Spirit; revealed to me in layers upon layers of my understanding; using the knowledge of scriptures that were deposited in me at the hearing of His word.

8. As each stage is revealed to you, like the headlights in a tunnel, you will have insight into who you need to become to move forwards to the next phase of your journey.

9. RECOGNISE your 'I AMs' as they propel you forwards to make your potential visible.

10. Whatever unique gifts you have, make them visible to the world. Mine them as you would gold, purposefully and persistently; and then shimmer like that gold.

11. Once you know what your real voice sounds like, it will stand out from the rest and no situation will affect its aim.

12. Use your unique voice and make it known.

13. Know that God has you and His outcome is in the palm of His hand. Place your trust in Him and He will never fail you.

That's how you *become* the difference so that you can be the difference.

16. The Beginning...

Reader, as I now part with you at this intersection, know that you are not alone. God's Spirit will continue to guide you to succeed in accordance with Him who looks upon the world as having one purpose. If you allow Him...

Your answer to this message will be proof of what you have allowed and thus learned. You are perfectly packaged just the way you are and in relinquishment of your judgements you will subconsciously give permission for others to do the same; so with faith; armed with your new perspective, go now and...

Be The Difference!

"Don't let the noise of others' opinions drown out your own inner voice. And most important, have the courage to follow your heart and intuition. They somehow already know what you truly want to become. Everything else is secondary." STEVE JOBS

WISDOM KEY

Receive your healing and own your difference!

Appendix

Appendix

GOD	HUMAN BEINGS
Truth	Untruth -Wrong/Right
The Whole Picture	Perspective
Ubiquitous	Unique – not everywhere
Vision	Sight
Real	Illusion/lie
Knowledge	Information
Knowing	Beliefs
Meaning	Meaningless
Oneness	Duality/Difference
Justice	Revenge

Definition of Perspective

1. The art of representing three-dimensional objects on a two-dimensional surface so as to give the right impression of their height, width, depth, and position in relation to each other.
   "the theory and practice of perspective"

2. A particular attitude towards or way of regarding something; a point of view.
   "most guidebook history is written from the editor's perspective"

Example of perspective
Perspective is the way that one looks at something. It is also an art technique that changes the distance or depth of an object on paper. An example of perspective is a farmer's opinion about lack of rain. An example of perspective is a painting where the railroad tracks appear to be curving into the distance.

Definition of Perception

1. The ability to see, hear or become aware of something through the senses.
   "the normal limits to human perception"

2. The way in which something is regarded, understood or interpreted.

Perception can be defined as the way you think about or understand someone or something. ... Your perception in life is determined by your past experiences, values, beliefs, and overall psychological makeup. In short, your perception is your reality. It is the way you see the world. It is your life

In addition to the five perceptions of sight, sound, touch, taste and smell, there is a field of psychology that studies Extrasensory Perception (ESP).

Example of perception
"Hollywood's perception of the tastes of the American public
1. Spend time alone

About the author

Valerie Alaeve Campbell is an enhanced relationship coach and a best-selling author. She speaks to millions worldwide via her weekly radio show - The Secret Vibe; effecting spiritual growth, particularly in the arena of dating.

Her spiritual teachings are based on 'love your neighbour as you love yourself, which she explains led to her study of the bible, law of attraction, spiritual psychotherapy (A course in Miracles) and the works of Byron Katie (Loving What Is) .

Her coaching business primarily started due to insights gained in her role as the only female managing in excess of 100 men over 10 years. It was there she learnt the influence of her feminine energy to compel her 'boys', unlike her fellow male counterparts to go over and beyond their line of duty.

Today she now teaches her secret vibe via various platforms to effect positive change in all areas of life. V.I.B.E is an acronym for vision/intention/beliefs/expectation.

Ms Campbell is of west-Indian parentage; she loves keeping fit, has a passion for dresses and resides as a mother and grandmother in London.

She can be contacted at
https://valerieacampbell.com/contact

Join her Facebook group at
https://www.facebook.com/groups/valerieacampbell

VALERIE A. CAMPBELL